CHRISTO SULLIVA

The HOUSE PLANT Book

FOR BEGINNERS

© Copyright 2021 - All rights reserved.
The content contained within this book may not be reproduced, duplicated or transmitted without direct writ- ten permission from the author or the publisher. Under no circumstances will any blame or legal responsibility be held against the publisher, or author, for any damages, reparation, or monetary loss due to the information contained within this book. Either directly or indirectly

Legal Notice:
This book is copyright protected. This book is only for personal use. You cannot amend, distribute, sell, use, quote or paraphrase any part, or the content within this book, without the consent of the author or publisher.

Disclaimer Notice:
Please note the information contained within this document is for educational and entertainment purposes only. All effort has been executed to present accurate, up to date, and reliable, complete information. No warranties of any kind are declared or implied. Readers acknowledge that the author is not engaging in the rendering of legal, financial, medical or professional advice. The content within this book has been derived from various sources. Please consult a licensed professional before attempting any techniques outlined in this book. By reading this document, the reader agrees that under no circumstances is the author responsible for any losses, direct or indirect, which are incurred as a result of the use of information contained within this document, including, but not limited to, errors, omissions, or inaccuracies.

TABLE OF CONTENT

INTRODUCTION	1
Make it Beautiful	3
Everything is better in three	5
Play with Texture	6
Houseplant Profile	9
MACULATA BEGONIA	10
AFRICAN VIOLET	13
AGLAONEMA	15
TILLANDSIA AIR PLANTS	18
ALOCASIA	21
ALOE BARBADENSIS	25
DYPSIS LUTESCENS	27
BIRD'S NEST FERN	29
BIRD OF PARADISE	32
BOSTON FERN	35
CACTUS	38
SCHLUMBERGERA BUCKLEYI	41
PLECTRANTHUS SCUTELLARIOIDES	44
MUSA	47
SCHLUMBERGERA GAERTNERI	50
ECHEVERIAS	53
KALA CHOE BLOSSFELDIANA	57
SPATHIPHYLLUM	60
HEDERA HELIX	62
JASMINUM POLYANTHUM	65

CRASSULA OVATA	67
JEWEL ORCHID	71
MONSTERA DELICIOSA	74
PHALAENOPSIS	77
CHRYSANTHEMUM MORIFOLIUM	79
EPIPREMNUM AUREUM	82
OXALIS	85
CHLOROPHYTUM	89
HOYA KERRII	91
TILLANDSIA	95
AECHMEA FASCIATA	97
TRADESCANTIA ZEBRINA	100
ZAMIOCULCAS ZAMIIFOLIA	102
CYCLAMEN PERSICUM	105
The World of Succulent	*108*
FRITHIA PULCHRA	116
SENECIO BARBARTONICUS	118
CRASSULA RUPESTRIS MARNERIANA	120
XEROSICYOS DANGUYI	123
CRASSULA	125
Repotting Houseplants	*129*
CONCLUSION	138
INDEX	**140**

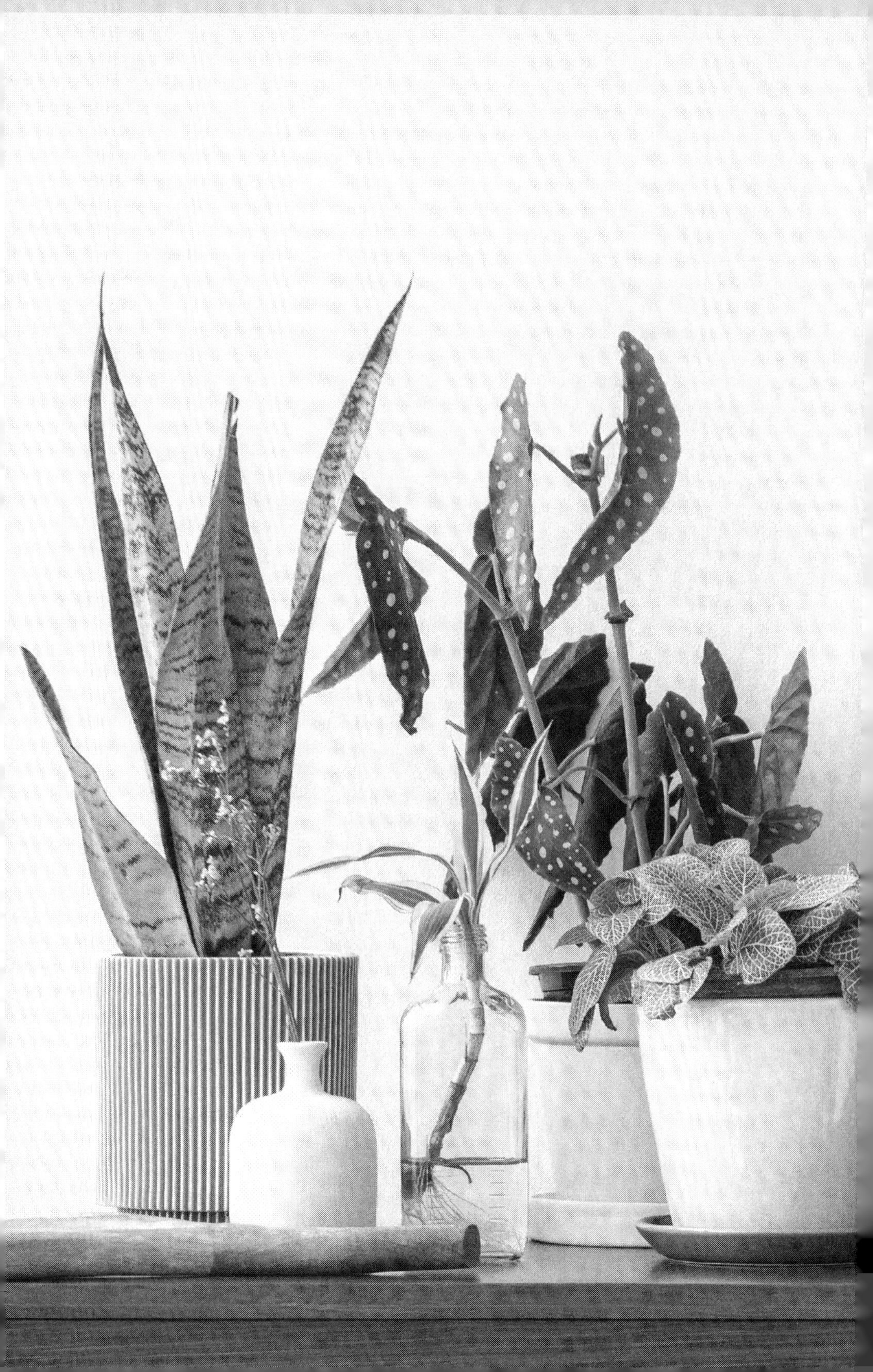

INTRODUCTION

This handbook is for you to have a comprehensive 360° view on what you can do and what you can't do when you're starting your journey in the houseplant realm.

My name is Christo Sullivan and this is my second contribution to the indoor gardening literature, namely the house plants, the wonderfully green friends that we can host in our houses and can help us to relax, shoo away stress, and reconnect with Nature, even if we are living in a busy and bustling city, or - as I call them - urban nightmare.

In this book I'm going to cut the fuss, and go directly to the nitty and gritty of the house plants domain: the plants.

You can practice indoor gardening as a passion, as a hobby, even as a profession, but the common denominator is to have fun, to use the company of our green companions as a happy relief-corner of our life. If you grow your plants in the right way - which means, with the right mindset - I promise you they will make you a plant enthusiast, if you're not one yet.

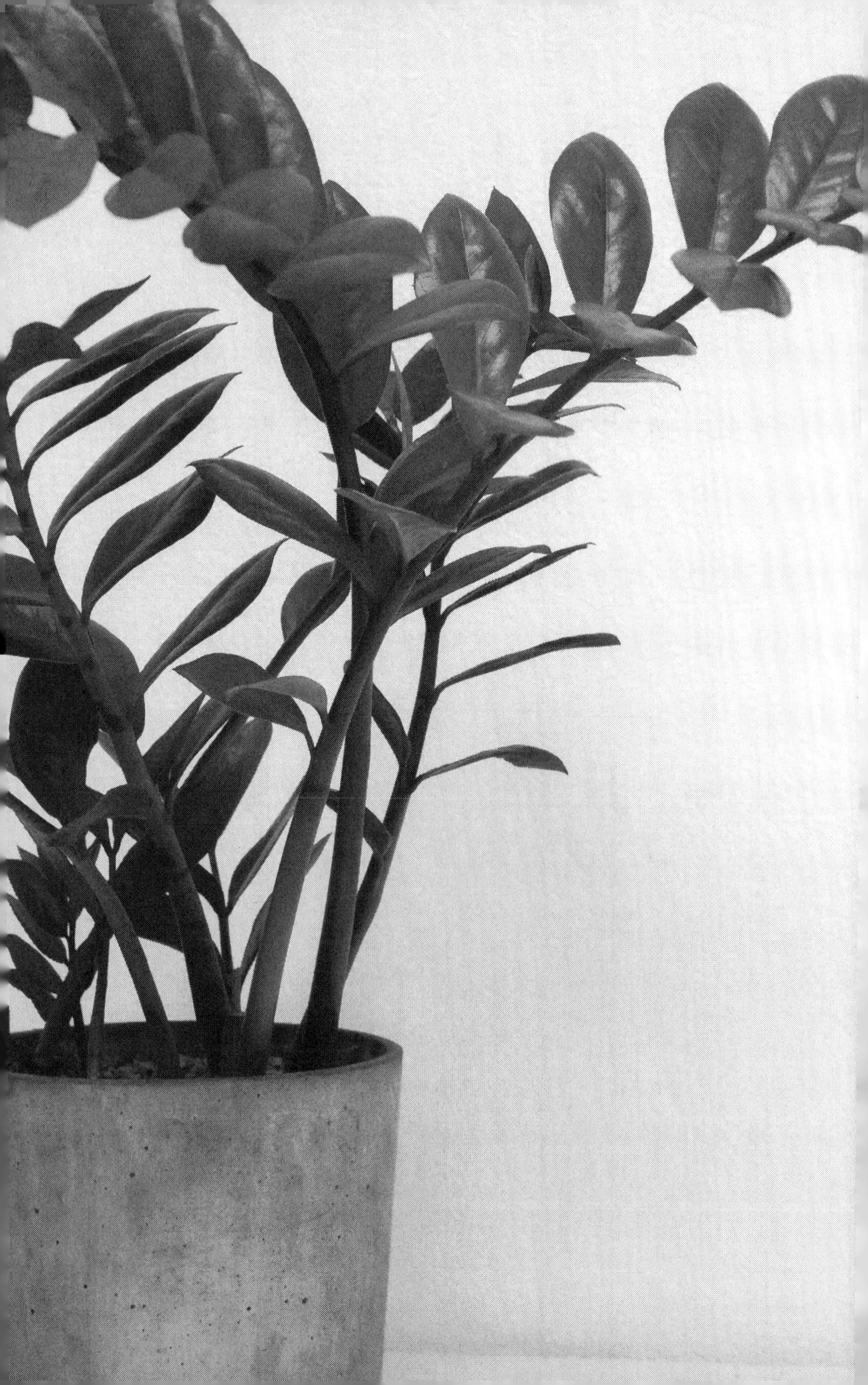

CHAPTER 1

Make it Beautiful

Indoor gardening is in fact a form of horticulture therapy in which the medicinal effects of indoor plants serve the contemporary women and men that need an assistance with everyday's life. As the term "indoor garden" indicates, it refers to a garden that can be built indoors. Indoor gardens are very democratic, as they can be built really anywhere, wether you live in villa, or a tiny flat, that you want to green-up a residential or commercial structure, such as hotels, hospitals, and business offices. Indoor plants are used to decorate all kinds of interior spaces.

This gives us a strong weapon, to embellish make any environment healthy for our body and our spirit too. And of course I am not forgetting the aesthetic part of the deal. How we arrange the plants in our houses matters, because it's where we live, so it makes only sense to use a little of sense of beauty (or what we consider so) and maximize our interiors. Indoor plants may be arranged in a variety of ways, either in appropriate combinations or as a single specimen item. There are some general rules, or better, guidelines that one could follow, for example, a group of large bold-leaved plants should be positioned against a large wall in a large space. On the other hand, single plant collections work well in small rooms. Tall plants, such as philodendrons and rubber plants, are better suited to rooms with horizontal lines, while tall monstera plants and big ferns are best suited to rooms with clear straight lines in a contemporary style. Ficus, diffenbachia, and dracaena are ideal for a classic style room with ornate furnishings. Or think an amaryllis or chrysanthemum plants with red, yellow, or orange flowers; they are ideal for rooms with a white or light colored backdrop. Plants with brightly colored leaves, such as coleus and caladium, can also work well in those spaces. And some things just ask for some logic and common sense: for instance plants with white flowers work well in rooms with dark backgrounds, but also plants with variegated leaves, such as caladium, will make a beautiful, yet more subtle, contrast.

If what you are after is a visual effect of he exploitation of the tridimensionality of a specific space, you should probably consider using ferns that can be easily grouped together to achieve a great effect, and if the group includes different varieties what is created is an even greater visual texture. If you want some color you should go for a group of different varieties of begonias that you can group together to achieve an explosion of colorful armony.

So you may understand how grouping can be a perfect combo for an augmented visual experience, when you have the right plant. Specific plant height must be taken into account when grouping indoor plants for dark corners of rooms. Tall plants are placed in the rear, medium tall plants in the center, and dwarf trailing plants in the front. Spacially, tall plants should be placed in the center of a hall or room, medium tall plants should be grouped around tall plants, and dwarf plants should be placed along the perimeter. I this way you're goin to give your "little forest" an harmonious beginning, middle, and end. Potted chrysanthemums, potted asters, potted coleus, and caladium are excellent choices for such arrangements. Plants grown in terrariums and glass cases, plants grown in bottles, cups, dishes and troughs, and aquarium cases are the best indoor plants for table decorations. Indoor plants may be used to create miniature gardens inside your home. Miniature landscapes such as forest scenes, desert scenes, and formal garden scenes can be produced using the right mix of vegetation and flowering plants. If you want to put in some scenographic effort, your imagination is your only limit. Indoor plants can be presented in stunning combinations, and can make any ambience of your house special: floors, window sills and ledges, tables and desks, book cases and book shelves, shelves and trolleys, window boxes or planters.

Everything is better in three

A well known rule of (green) thumb for styling any space is to avoid grouping items together in even numbers. An even number transmits symmetry, which often brings a degree of formality which in my experience is seldom the most adapt to a home where you want to live and relax. The best way to group plants together is in odd numbers, 3, 5, 7… Or just one single plant that make a corner or a coffee table precious in its simplicity. For the same reason you should generally avoid grouping plants with the same, uniform, height. This conformation will cause the plants to blend together taking out of each plant its uniqueness. My suggestion is to include at least one plant in each group which is considerably taller than the others. Another useful advice about grouping is to try to put together plants which have something in common, a salient visual quality such as the color of their leaves, their density, their direction. Having a common visual theme adds to the natural feeling of the bunch, avoiding the risk to look randomly put together.

This is something that is often ignored, but can make a huge difference in the visual. The texture of the leaves, their physical composition, plays a subtle but substantial role in the general impression you can have of a corner of a living room if the plants used in a group varies in structure and consistency. When two plants or two version of the same plants are paired, it's important to think in terms of contrast, such as rough versus smooth or detailed versus minimal.

Play with Texture

The advice here is, if you have minimalistic interiors, a plant with a more intricate appearance, with many peculiar details that can be noticed even fro afar, will make the ambience multi-dimensional, so that we can appreciate both the two contrasting style together. An example of plant to obtain this could be Maranta Leuconeira or a Zanzibar Gem. If, on the other hand, your house is already full of texture and detailed garnishes a plain yet elegant big glossy leaf is what you should go for in order to regain the room's balance, like the elegant Red Congo.

Something else you have control upon arranging plants is the "flatness" of a room. Depending on the height of your plants you have the freedom to explore the eye level or higher. Taller plants are usually displayed o the ground level, while smaller plants can be placed on a shelf or hanging from the ceiling, giving you the chance to use the space also in its verticality. On a shelf for example one of the best thing you can have is a trailing plant, like a cascading photos; it's vines will grow out to create an abundant jungle-like feel. You can also use plant stands to help the plant look to stand out in its vertical, especially when its color is contrasting.

The single trait that I deem the most important in the houseplants in a room however, especially for that first glance that you throw to a room when you first enter it, is… the direction of where the leaves grow. Using the leading lines of a plant's leaves is a great way to lead direction toward a retina area of the room. There are some plants whose leaves point naturally to the ceiling, and lead the eye up, like the famous snake plant. On the contrary, the eye is drawn downward by pants with trailing vines, like those within the photos and Philodendron families. Their mantles are perfect to bring attention to a fireplace or any other key furniture piece.

Lastly, try to balance the colors in your room with that of your plants. If you have a group of three plants you may want to try a primary color, a secondary color and the smallest of them with a vivid bold color, to add just a splash of sparkly note, for example with a fluorescent - and contained - yellow. Or what about the pink details of a rubber tree?
A different discussion should be made about the vase, containers or planters that you're going to use. Also them play a relevant role, and you can play around with the many different options that you can find on the market.

The last fundamental piece of advice is that no plant is as beautiful as a thriving plant. The most important thing you can do for your plants to look good, is to treat them in the proper way. Make them happy, and they'll make you happy as well.

CHAPTER 2
Houseplant Profile

You can't wait to start your journey into the houseplants world. I can't blame you. In fact I believe you have already started one. The greens are in the house. So, what's next? You want your plants to thrive, how do you make it happen? First, you have to determine what kind of plant do you have. Depending on the plant type you have purchased - or that you are about to buy - the condition of light, watering, climate, how it grows and how it can be repotted, may change. From here you can determine what's the best way to care for it. What follows is a list of what I consider the best plants you can take care of if you're not an expert, but you still want to fill your house with plants. Easy enough, but at the same time beautiful, curious, and make great decoration for your house.

If you're new to plant caring, this is a perfect place to start. If you've been caring for plants for a while, this could be a good refresher. Here we go.

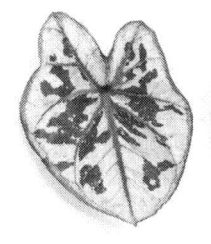

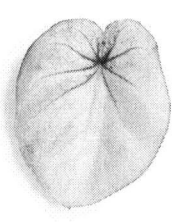

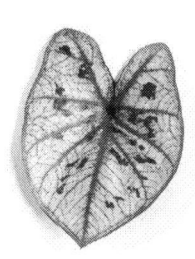

MACULATA BEGONIA

(Indoor Polkadot Plant)

Polka dot Begonia, the maculata, is a real eyecatcher.

Place it on a design table, or against a backdrop with geometrical or minimalistic features, and with its large olive green angel wing-shaped leaves patterned with polka dots on top and a deep purple-red on the bottom side, it will draw on her everybody's attention. The best part is that with this houseplant, you don't need a green thumb to impress. They are very permissive and will live with little or no effort on your part.

Begonia plants come in a variety of styles, heights, and shapes, as well as hybrids. The Begonia maculata is a fast-growing plant that makes a great indoor houseplant or terrarium plant, and is without a doubt one of the most beautiful Begonia plants I've ever seen, that's why she's the first of our list.

TRUST ME: get one and you will already feel halfway on your path to become a plant-expert

Indoor Polkadot Plant Care Guide

LIGHT

Bright, indirect sunlight is ideal for Begonia maculata. It is possible for her, however, to expand also in low-light conditions. Keep the plant out of the intense early afternoon sun; the leaves of the polka dot begonia will burn and dry out if they are exposed to too much sunlight.

While light is essential, the humidity factor is the key to begonia maculata treatment. Its native habitat is a steamy setting, which doesn't mean you will need to build a greenhouse for it, but you will have to allow for some humidity to keep your maculata happy and healthy. A sad clown begonia is the last thing anyone needs.

WATERING

Since the Begonia maculata don't like to be left dry for long periods of time, it should be watered on a daily basis. It prefers a damp soil setting, keep an eye out, however, for soggy seeds, which won't help the plant's well-being at all. Becasue of that, before watering, let the top of the soil dry out. Let it drain in full before placing the pot back on the saucer or in its cache pot.

The Begonia maculata may need to be watered more often when it is vigorously growing in the spring and summer, as the temperatures are higher and the sun rays intake is much more.

In the winter, it can be challenging to understand their watering needs. Simply water your begonia less and less often while checking the soil. The Begonia maculata does not go dormant in the winter, but it does slow down considerably. It still needs to be watered though, so make sure to keep on watering it regularly also during he winter. Don't let your good intentions hurt your beautiful plant; learn to listen her.

FLOWERING

You can find blooms on a single stem from spring to fall, that will tend to form clusters of white flowers with cheery yellow centers. Just beautiful, and one of my wife's favorites.

REPOTTING

Since this plant tends to be root attached, the best growing condition for it would be in a smaller container. Don't be tempted to repot it too fast because it thrives in small spaces.

When it's time to repot, do so in the spring when the plant is only starting to expand and will be ready to fit into its new container. Make sure the new pot is one size larger than the old one and has drainage holes to save the plant from getting root rot.

AFRICAN VIOLET

Since it is native to Africa and the flowers resemble violets (though they are unrelated), the Saintpaulia houseplant is also known as the African Violet. This plant is a relatively recent addition to our homes, having first appeared in vast quantities in America in the 1930s, but it has been well-received ever since.

African violets are among the most common houseplants in the world, and for good reason. These low-growing, compact plants bloom several times a year and come in a variety of leaf shapes and colors. Don't let their reputation for complexity deter you: African violets will excel indoors if you follow a few basic guidelines.

TRUST ME: *With a little practice, you can keep them in bloom almost all year and raise them to be the size of dinner plates.*

African Violet Care Guide

LIGHT

Always keep your African Violet out of direct sunshine. If you want to make flowers, you'll need a lot of sun. The plant will move to a shadier place, but this will result in a longer time between flowering periods.

WATERING

Enable the compost to dry out somewhat between watering to keep it moist. While many people recommend only watering from the bottom, if you are smart, you should water from the tip. Slow down so you don't splash the leaves, which will spoil their velvety appearance and greatly raise the risk of multiple fungal infections.

HUMIDITY

The plant prefers high humidity, but you should avoid misting it to increase humidity in case it's too low, since this will often damp the leaves way too much. Instead, try some of our other suggestions to avoid problems caused by too-wet leaves.

FERTILIZING

Use a high-potash feed if possible, or an all-purpose houseplant variety if that isn't possible. If you decide to enrich your household with African Violet flowers, you'll need to feed them every couple of weeks. Reduce the feeding schedule if you are not supplying the required bright (but indirect) light so the plant would not need it. Temperatures the Violet is comfortable in range from 60°F to 72°F (15°C to 21°C). In the winter, try to maintain the temperature above 60°F / 15°C.

REPOTTING

Again, don't go on a repotting spree. If you do it too often, you may reduce the flowering capacity, as a slightly plant-bound pot aids in the blooming process. Repotting is needed for very young plants or mature plants that are too pot-bound, preferably in the spring or early summer.

AGLAONEMA

(Chinese Evergreens)

Aglaonema, or Chinese Evergreens, are decorative foliage houseplants that flourish in our homes and offices. They're great for beginners because they tolerate low light and intermittent maintenance, but they're still appealing to seasoned gardeners.

True, they don't have the same wow factor as some other indoor plants, but Chinese Evergreens are incredibly understated, and they're one of the best plants to make every office more relaxed with a touch of elegance. In fact they are a great addition to any classic style home. They grow slowly and take a long time to outgrow their containers, so they need little upkeep. They're tough and, for the most part, laid-back. In reality, they're among the least fussy houseplants available.

TRUST ME: *Aglaonema plants in general are extremely adaptable to a wide range of indoor environmental growth conditions.*

Indoor Polkadot Plant Care Guide

LIGHT

These plants are ideal for mild, medium, and bright light environments in your house. They'll add a splash of color and flourish in places where other houseplants could suffer. They won't live in complete darkness, so don't even think about placing it in a room with no windows.

According to conventional wisdom, Aglaonema species with light green or highly variegated foliage need more light than those with darker green and less variegation. You won't go wrong if you follow this rule.

WATERING

These plants prefer a slightly damp / moist soil. So don't allow it to neither be wet soil or go completely dry. In the winter, if your plant is in a low-light setting, you can only need to water it once every two weeks. Watering once or twice a week might be needed in lighter light or if the temperature is extremely hot.

While these plants are very low maintenance, there's a possibility for things to go wrong by mistake when it comes to watering. These are the symptoms to watch for and what they mean.

- Drooping leaves and wet soil meanshe plant is over-watered.
- Leaves and stems pointing very upright along with dry soil mean the plant is under-watered.

HUMIDITY

Since these plants are tough, if given the option, they would choose high humidity, but they can also cope with low humidity. They won't thrive if the air in your home or office is very dry, so keep that in mind.

REPOTTING AND SOIL

Plants of the genus Aglaonema mature slowly and compactly. As a result, they take a long time to outgrow a pot. Of course, this will happen naturally, but if the plant seems to be particularly congested or hasn't produced new growth in a long time, it's probably time to repot it.

They'll thrive in a number of growing mediums, so you can probably use anything you already have on hand. If you're buying something new, it'll probably be cheaper and easier to stick to the basics and opt for something labelled for houseplants or garden plants.

TILLANDSIA AIR PLANTS

This little plant is a beauty, and as a low-maintenance houseplant, Tillandsia Air Plants are quickly gaining popularity. They don't need to be grown in soil pots because they have such a small root system. Air Plants may be hung, mounted, or set in terrariums, bottle gardens, or other decorative containers with grit, stones, or pretty much anything else. Air plants are ideal for craft designs, small-space living, and ultimately, bragging rights for brown-thumb gardeners. Superglue their roots to stones or wood, or tuck them into shells and driftwood crevices, glass baubles, and wire baskets. Place them between the leaves or around the base of your larger houseplants. They make ideal companions for orchids, cactus and bromeliads. Alternatively, simply place them unadorned on a sunny windowsill or shelf.

Air Plant Care Guide

LIGHT

According to popular belief, all Air Plants need bright light with a little direct sunlight every now and then. However, depending on the variety, I've discovered that Air Plants can thrive under a variety of light conditions. The natural color of the Air Plant is a good starting point. The color spectrum begins with dark green and progresses through light green, grey, and finally to almost white variations.

The green ones would do well in places with little sun, all the way up to some bright spots on window ledges. They don't like direct sunshine, though.

WATERING

Watering Air Plants can be done in two ways. The first step is to mist the leaves two or three times a week. If the plant is set in place which is difficult to reach this is a good option.

Dunk your Air Plant in a bottle with room temperature water as a second choice. Some argue that a dunk is insufficient and that the plant should be soaked in the container for at least half hour.

I don't really disagree, particularly if you live in a dry climate or your plant is severely dehydrated. However, soaking it in this manner on a daily basis makes caring for these plants even more complex and time intensive than it needs to be.

Instead, I think that dunking them in the container for no longer than 15 seconds before extracting them and shaking off the excess water, makes them completely content.

It's crucial to shake off any extra water to have enough time for the plant to fully dry before nightfall as the temperature decreases. There is a risk of decay if there is too much moisture on the plant and the temperature lowers. As a general rule, water early in the morning rather than late at night.

HUMIDITY

This may be crucial. Dark to light green air plants need more regular watering and a higher humidity level than grey air plants.

You should be good if you can mist or soak once or twice a week, and you should be able to ignore humidity. If watering that much is a challenge for you, the humidity must be kept at a reasonable level to keep the balance.

REPOTTING

The wonderful trait of not having any sort of extensive root system means this is one of the very few houseplants that will never need repotting.

Speed of Growth. The Tillandsia grow rapidly at first, but then it slows down, state that will persist for the remainder of the plant's life. Whatever you do for your Tillandsia, don't expect it to grow quickly.

ALOCASIA

(Kris Plant / Elephant Ear)

The Kris Plant, Elephant Ear, and African Mask Plant are both names for Alocasia. This unusual-looking houseplant will occasionally bloom, but it's usually not bought for that purpose. The peculiarity of the Alocasia is all about the rare and alien-like leaves.

Look at them, they will make any ambience special. The striking leaves are arrowhead or shield shaped, with long protruding white veins running across them, which contrast sharply with the dark green leaf.

Alocasia Care Guide

Alocasia is not tough to grow, but it is probably one of the most demanding plant in this list, because ti will not tolerate poor treatment or poor conditions over extended periods of time.

LIGHT

You should keep your plant out of direct sunlight as well as from places that are very dark and gloomy. It is important to find locations that are halfway between these two extremes. In our experience, two species of Alocasia, Zebrina and Mycorrhiza, cope much better with morning or late afternoon sun dropping on their leaves than the Amazonica species, that deals better with extended exposure to sunlight.

WATERING

When the compost is in active development, it must be kept moist at all times. That's not dry or soggy; it's sticky. The roots of the Elephant Plant hate being dry, but too much water can cause them to rot.

Rather than following traditional houseplant watering advice, we've discovered that the best approach is to water little. If you want to reserve her a special trearment, make an attempt to use tepid rainwater if possible.

HUMIDITY

Another explanation for this plant's growing failure in a home setting is the lack of moisture in the air. It's a tropical plant that needs moderate to high humidity.

REPOTTING

Repotting in the spring isn't always needed, but if your plant has developed a lot of offsets or has outgrown its container, it could be a good idea. While they seem to be tropical and unique species, you can use any regular houseplant compost or blend.

SPEED OF GROWTH

In summer, when the days are long and the temperature is high, expect a moderate rate of development. One new leaf each month is reasonably normal; marginally less is also acceptable and not cause for concern. If you have not spot any new leaves in 6 months, you can consider repotting or fertilizing (if you haven't already).

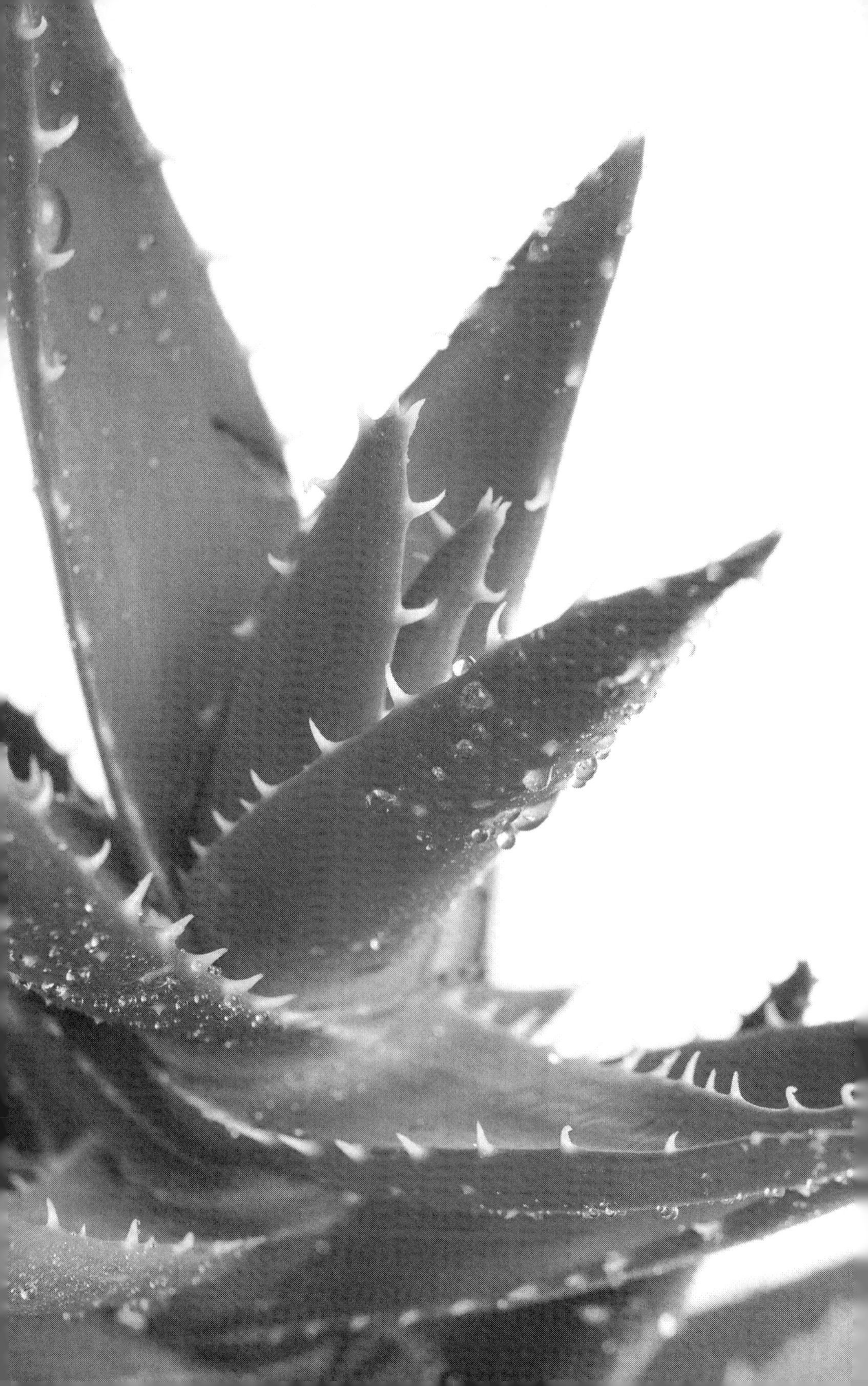

ALOE BARBADENSIS

(Aloe Vera)

Because of the Aloe Vera gel found within its leaves, the Aloe Barbadensis plant is one of the most well-known houseplants.

Aloe vera is a well-known medicinal plant that has been used by humans for thousands of years. It includes antioxidant and antibacterial elements as well as beneficial plant compounds. If you want to improve your health, you may even grow them and learn to extract the Aloe substance. I suggest that you try and bring half a glass of it every morning, You'd be surprised of the benefits.

Aloe Vera Care Guide

LIGHT

Your Aloe Vera plant will thrive in every South-facing window because it will get plenty of sunlight. It's simply built for such places, like most succulents, and as a result, you'll get good quality leaves and an even growth.

However, Aloes will resist also in a north-facing location; only, growth will be slower, and you'll need to change the plant pot every month or two to maintain an even appearance. When it comes to light, the Aloe Vera plant is generally adaptable, and once it's growing it's very difficult to stop.

WATERING

During the spring and summer, water thoroughly if the soil becomes dry. The location of the plant will determine how long it takes for the soil to dry out and, as a result, how long you would go between waterings. It's perfectly normal to wait anywhere from a week to three weeks.

In hot weather, aloes can use a lot of water, so don't be afraid to water them. Water less often in the Fall and Winter. Some people don't water their plants at all during the winter, which, if they're in a particularly cool place, is usually a smart thing to avoid root/stem rot. During winter your Aloe will start to suffer only if temperature goes below 30F.

HUMIDITY

Almost all succulents, including the Aloe Vera vine, do not need much humidity.

REPOTTING

Aloe Vera plants typically grow a large number of offsets or suckers in a short period of time, eventually filling the jar. When the pot gets overcrowded, repot.

If you want a "busy" look, hold all of the plants together in a larger container, or separate any of the offsets for propagation or gifting.

SPEED OF GROWTH

In ideal conditions, your Aloe Vera plant can grow at a moderate pace. If conditions are bad, and, of course, during the winter months when everything slows down, expect very little development.

HEIGHT / SPREAD

They are usually just 45cm / 18in high. However, because of the offsets that fan out around, if you one day decide to plant it outside, in that case the spread (over several years) can be enormous.

DYPSIS LUTESCENS

(Areca Palm / Butterfly Palm)

The Areca Palm, also known as the Butterfly Palm, is a low-maintenance houseplant which has a lot to offer. This lovely Nature's masterpiece has earned the "Royal Horticultural Society's Award of Garden Merit", which is quite an accomplishment for a plant that is more widely grown indoors than outdoors. Because of its narrow, multiple fronds spaced close to one another in tidy compact lines along the stems, it can easily be distinguished from other varieties of palms. It's an "airy" plant that can give you the impression of an elegant urban forest; 3 or 4 of them lined in two rows can really give a pleasant tridimensional look to the green in your house.

Areca Palm Care Guide

LIGHT

Areca palms can grow in a spot that receives no sunshine at all during the day as well as one which is exposed to direct sunlight, but they don't like excessive quantities of either. It's best to stay away from very dim shady areas and constant direct sunshine. The best possible position we can place it is a spot which is sunny, but that gets no direct sunlight; or alternatively a spot that receives just a limited amount of direct light during the morning or the evening.

WATERING

Areca Palms are tropical native plants, and they're genetically used to frequent tropical rains, and to having their roots in perpetually moist soil. And this is exactly how we should keep them when we choose to keep this plant in our homes: we will need to keep the soil moist for long periods of time. This palm is thirsty in the spring, summer, and autumn/fall, necessitating frequent and heavy watering especially throughout the summer. If the location you have selected for the Areca is really hot, you might need to water it twice a week. Despite its thirst for moisture, too much water can easily destroy your plant. It's better to wait until the surface soil has dried before watering again. An occasional draught can be tolerated by the plant, but you should not keep its soil dry for more than a couple days.

REPOTTING

Since palms dislike constant root disturbance, frequent repotting will harm your Areca and prevent its growth. However, since they don't grow very quickly and don't like being in smaller pots with their roots crowded, repotting isn't something you should be doing very often. I'd say once every couple of years is enough, but if your plant happens to be very young, as it grows you'll be repotting it once a year in the Spring, before it matures. When it comes to doing it, regular potting soil would suffice.

HEIGHT / SPREAD

It can reach generous height, but few indoor specimens would ever grow to be more than 10 ft (3 m) tall.

BIRD'S NEST FERN

(Asplenium Nidus)

Asplenium nidus, or Bird's Nest Fern, is one of many common and attractive ferns that can be easily grown as houseplants. Ferns such as this one thrive next to windows facing North, which is the best one for its quality of light and correct average temperature.

The Bird's Nest Fern will reward you with a large number of naturally glossy leaves arranged in a circular pattern that resembles a bird's nest (hence the common name for these houseplants)

Bird Nest Fern Care Guide

LIGHT

The Bird's Nest Fern needs only medium light levels to grow strong, which makes it more durable in less warmer enviroments. If you have a North-facing windows you should have one of this plant in front of it.

If you don't have such a spot or if your rooms don't face North, just keep it out of the sunlight and you'll be fine.

WATERING

You should not allow the soil to dry out at all during the growing process; instead, keep it only damp.

The first reason why ferns often die in homes is the way they are watered, either too much or too little. Although an occasional mistake is appropriate, you can continue to work with your Fern by keeping the soil just moist during the growing seasons (Spring, Summer, and Autumn/Fall).

HUMIDITY

The plant needs a high level of humidity to survive, which is why it thrives in humid terrariums, sunrooms, and conservatories.

Of course, you can grow a smaller plant without specialized equipment. Just know that id the ambience is dry you should add a humidifier somewhere near your plant.

REPOTTING

When the thin roots entirely fill the existing jar, it's time to repot; if this happens, it's time to transfer it to a somewhat larger tub. If you don't, the growth will slow down and finally end.

A young Bird Nest Fern plant should be repotted once a year until it reaches a good height (around 1.5ft), after which it should only need repotting every couple of years.

You don't need to use or do something overly fancy while you're repotting your fern. Standard potting soil will do, and if the roots are very compacted, gently loosen them with your fingertips.

HEIGHT / SPREAD

After several years, a maximum height of 4ft / 120cm and a spread of 3ft / 90cm can be achieved, but only in a very humid climate. Half these size

BIRD OF PARADISE

(Strelitzia)

The spectacular, unmistakable, and unchallenged Queen of the houseplant world is the Strelitzia, also known as the Bird of Paradise Plant. When it's in bloom, the flowers resemble the head of an exotic crested duck, which is how it got its common name.

Sunbirds pollinate the flowers by perching on the "beak" ledge of the flower. The weight of the bird on the "beak" opens it, allowing pollen to fall onto the bird and be deposited on the next flower it visits. Just magical.

Bird of Paradise Care Guide

LIGHT

You'll need bright light and some sun if you want a lot of growth and this wonderful plant's flowers. A window with an east or west orientation should suffice. It's also a good idea to choose a south-facing window if you want some protection from the hot summer sun, which can roast the leaves of immature plants.

North-facing location should be avoided if you plan to keep the Strelitzia there for a long time. It will tolerate a darker location for a while, but in that case its development will be much slower, and flowering unlikely. So the best solution is to give her some south-facing exposure initially, and place it next to an east or west facing window When the plant is strong enough.

WATERING

The amount of water required will be determined by the location of your plant. Plants in lighter, colder locations would need significantly more than those in darker locations. The usual reasonable rule of thumb - watering when the surface of the soil turns dry - is valid here. I have 3 Strelitzia and one tip I use to understand if they have enough water is one that you can use with any plant that can stay in a small pot: lift it and "feel" its weight. After a while you will develop a feel for when to water just by the weight of the pot. The less the water I the pots, the lighter they will be.

HUMIDITY

If the air is very dry, a light misting can help to remove the dust that collects on the leaves. For my experience humidity is not an essential condition for this plant to grow.

REPOTTING

When the Strelitzia is young, it is perfectly fine to repot each Spring using normal potting compost. However if you want flowers or you're trying to restrict the growth of the plant you need to keep it pot-bound. If it's housed in a plastic pot, a large Bird of Paradise will eventually distort and bulge it horribly. As a result, be prepared to cut it loose while repotting, and be aware that doing so would most likely interrupt the flowering period.

SPEED OF GROWTH

In ideal conditions, Bird of Paradise growth is rapid, with one new leaf appearing per month during the growing season. While it does not seem to be anything at first glance, the dense roots under the soil surface are genuinely thick and can quickly fill a pot, making this a fast-growing plant.

BOSTON FERN

(Nephrolepis Exaltata 'Bostoniensis')

The Boston Fern is a perfect plant to keep indoors to recalls the nature outside. A variety of Nephrolepis is a good choice if you want a dependable and relatively easy-to-care-for fern.
The Boston Fern has elegant green, drooping fronds that are naturally shaped in such a way that they seem ruffled, making it look great in a hanging basket or anywhere the fronds can hang down from, such as the edge of a bookcase or shelf.

Boston ferns (Nephrolepis exaltata) are now common houseplants because of their tridimensionality and the joy they can bring to a living room or a kitchen. Place it on a coffee table and they will lighten the room up right away.

Boston Fern Care Guide

LIGHT

It is important to provide adequate lighting. A Boston Fern can tolerate both full sun and partial shade, but for a happy and good-looking plant, choose a sunny spot that does not receive direct sunshine.

A window that faces north will be perfect. If looking east (or west in a pinch) is also appropriate, facing south in direct sunlight should be avoided.

WATERING

In the winter the soil should be almost always damp, just spray when its surface is dry. In hot weather, on the other hand, you may comfortably water this plant several days a week.

Moisture is essential, but don't overwater to the point that the soil becomes saturated and sodden. If you can, use rain water, but if it isn't possible, tap water would suffice. Only make sure it's been able to stay for an hour at room temperature, as very cold water will shock the roots.

REPOTTING

Repot only if you want the plant to grow larger, and even then, only after the roots have fully filled the original container. Make a special effort to keep the fern at the same soil level as before. It's important not to bury the crown, as this would make it rot and lead the plant to its inevitable demise.

SPEED OF GROWTH

When conditions are favorable, expect fast and consistent development for the majority of the year. In colder temperatures, or in case the roots have run out of room to develop, growth can considerably slow down.

HEIGHT / SPREAD

After several years, this fern can reach a maximum height of 3ft / 90cm and a spread of 6ft / 180cm.

CACTUS

(Desert Cacti)

Here is one of the plants that I suggest most often to people asking me what plant should they get to keep at home with no, or little, effort. The Desert Cacti have the same lighting, humidity, and watering specifications as other cacti. They never outgrow their spot in your home or their pots, are inexpensive to buy (when young), and only require simple care.

When compared to other houseplants, even if your thumb doesn't look anything like green and you are an undercover houseplants killer, a cactus will usually take more blows before succumbing. On the other hand, if you pay close attention, you will have a lovely peaceful companion rising happily, and maybe producing some lovely flowers.

Cactus Care Guide

LIGHT

In the vast majority of instances, a cactus can thrive in a position that enjoys direct sunshine for half or most part of the day. If your cactus can bloom indoors it will with this kind of light, but not all of them do. Almost all cacti, though, will tolerate a shadier spot for a while, but their growth will suffer. Think where they come from, shower them with light.

WATERING

The most frequent cactus misconception is that "they don't need much water". From one point of view, yes, this is absolutely correct; no other plant is as well suited to withstand prolonged drought. If you fail to water the soil after it has dried out, it will most likely live for several weeks, if not months, without damage, which makes it so versatile.

However, the plant has now become a survivor rather than a thriver as a result of this. Instead, the perfect time to water your cactus is when the soil has fully dried out from the last watering. When this occurs, re-water thoroughly and then stop giving until the soil has dried out again.

REPOTTING

Despite their ultimate size, most cacti have a small root volume relative to what can be seen above ground. Since the roots of small plants are mostly shallow rather than deep, using a wide container for them to "build into" is often a mistake, since it greatly raises the chance of overwatering and rotting.

Every year or so, young plants would need to be repotted to give the roots room to mature. You will reduce the frequency to 3 or 5 years cycles until it reaches a significant scale. For a very tall or mature cactus, you'll need a good solid and heavy container to keep it from toppling over. Many cactus growers suggest clay pots because they are porous and allow the roots to "breathe," but you can use plastic if you prefer. If you're repotting a cactus on a regular basis, make sure it gets fertilized.

ARE CACTUS PLANTS POISONOUS?

There are several different types of cacti to choose from, and some of them are toxic to both humans and pets. If they have thorns, claws, or spines, though, they shouldn't be a concern so you can keep curious children and pets safe (it's obviously advisable to not touch them).

SCHLUMBERGERA BUCKLEYI

(Christmas Cactus/Thanksgiving cactus)

The Christmas cactus is a very popular houseplant for a reason: they grow bright, tubular beautiful flowers in pink or lilac colors when they bloom. They're a fantastic plant because of their lovely flowers, long bloom time, and low maintenance requirements. I'm sure you'd love a Christmas cactus in your house!

Christmas Cactus Care Guide

LIGHT

The Christmas Cactus, unlike desert cacti, is native to shady forests. This ensures that clear, bright sunlight should be avoided, otherwise the leaves could turn to a reddish, almost damaged color. They need a well-lit area, but they may accept darker conditions if clearer light can be provided for at least a few months of the year. Direct sunlight must be avoided, which is unusual for cacti.

WATERING

Like all cacti they can store water in their thick fleshy leaves and rely on it in times of drought. However, if you want your specimen to thrive, you'll need to water it like a regular houseplant, anytime the soil becomes dry. Water the plant thoroughly and wait until the top inch or so of soil has dried out before watering it again. I've never seen one of these plants succumb to root rot as a result of overwatering, so they seem to be resistant to root rot, but I would avoid overwatering just in case.

TEMPERATURE

The average temperature present in most households shouldn't be a problem for our plant. After it has flowered, it needs to rest at a somewhat colder temperature, between 7°C and 16°C (45°F and 61°F). In most cases, an unheated space would be preferable. Sub-zero temperatures can be avoided at all costs.

REPOTTING

The Christmas Cactus grows steadily and takes a long time (years and years!) to become pot bound. If necessary, repot after flowering, but you shouldn't have to do it more than once every three years or so.
When it's time to repot it, just use a similar potting mix to the one it's currently in. This should be something relatively "open", such as regular potting soil or something specifically labelled for cactus and succulent plants. Since the root system is usually simple and not excessively vigorous, choose a pot that is only marginally larger than the previous one if you're also removing the growing container.

SPEED OF GROWTH

As houseplants, these plants mature at a slow pace. However, if the conditions are favorable, they will continue to grow at a reasonable rate, and you will see a lot of fresh light green growth in the growing season.

ARE CHRISTMAS PLANTS POISONOUS?

Although the leaves and flowers are unpleasant to the taste, the plant is not poisonous to humans, cats, or dogs.

PLECTRANTHUS SCUTELLARIOIDES

(Coleus Blumei)

Coleus Blumei hybrids, also known as Painted Nettles or Plectranthus scutellarioides in Latin, are historically cultivated as outdoor bedding plants that are handled as annuals. This ensures they're planted outdoors in late spring in order to embellish your garden during the summer and autumn, before succumbing to the frost.

If you haven't figured it out yet, the biggest selling point for these plants is the exquisitely brightly coloured and stunning leaves, some of which are marked with almost contrasting psychedelic patterns.

Coleus Care Guide

LIGHT

Coleus plants need a bright light source without direct sunlight to keep their markings, and since the leaf markings is the peculiar trait that makes this plant particularly appealing, it's critical that you get the light requirements right. Sitting squarely in a North, East, or West facing window is ideal, but, if the sunshine is filtered, you might be able to get away with a South facing window too.

Choose a bright light source that is warmed by the sun for best results.

WATERING

If you've picked a sunny spot that is automatically warmed by day light, you'll now need to keep the soil moist at all times, which might mean taking out your watering can once or twice a week. In the winter, cut back on irrigation and let the soil dry out a bit.

TEMPERATURE

Provide an average temperature of no less than 50°F (10°C), or the Coleus will perish.

REPOTTING

If you want to hold the plant alive through the winter, prune it back hard in the spring and repot it with fresh quality potting soil. You can keep the previous pot: unless you wish to maximize its total capacity, a size change is rarely necessary.

SPEED OF GROWTH

In optimal conditions, the growth rate is always very high, so you'll need to prune it on constantly to keep it compact and tidy.

HEIGHT/SPREAD

The stems will rise to 1ft - 2ft / 30cm - 60cm if left unchecked. This may be what you're aiming for but pinching out the growing tips on a regular basis will keep things shorter.

IS COLEUS POISONOUS?

Many hybrids are safe to have around people and livestock, but other varieties retain more of the "natural" characteristics of older plants. These have higher levels of essential oils in the leaves, which can induce vomiting and diarrhea if eaten in large quantities.

MUSA

(Banana Dwarf Cavendis)

Musa, also known as the banana, is one of the most well-known fruits in the world; in addition to being tasty and nutritious, several varieties can be cultivated as houseplants with ease and success.

Dwarf banana plants are often seen growing in areas of Asia for mass production, and they are often cultivated as tall demonstration plants in gardens at the back of borders to add a tropical touch. However, since they need a lot of care during winters, the average gardener is unlikely to cultivate them this way. It can seem unusual as a houseplant, but it has been grown indoors since Victorian days, when it was proudly displayed in their humid, wet, and sunny conservatories. Of course, Victorian conservatories were different (and somewhat larger) than the ones we have today, but the core concept remains the same.

TRUST ME: *This is a plant that will take everybody's attention.*

Banana Dwarf Care Guide

LIGHT

The Common Banana requires bright light, but it can tolerate a wide variety of lighting conditions, from partial shade to full sun. In full Summer sun, young plants and new leaves can scorch, particularly if your watering routine is not constant.

WATERING

During the hottest months of the year, a well-established Banana plant would need much more watering than most house plants, particularly in the Spring and Autumn/Fall. This is due to the wide leaf surface area, which makes for a great deal of transpiration, which is beneficial in the dry environment of a centrally heated home.

When the top 2 inches / 4cm of compost is dry, water it. You might be doing this as well as any other day in Summer if you're in a really light, warm place. However, if you don't cut back significantly in the winter, it's an invitation for rot to take over.

HUMIDITY

The leaves seem sturdy, but they are extremely fragile and can quickly rip if the right conditions are not met. Low humidity is a common cause of leaf destruction, so moisture-retentive pellets in the drip tray, as well as daily misting, will be beneficial.

FEEDING

Because this plant has big leaves that form quickly during the growing season, a new leaf every 10 days isn't unusual, and feeding on a regular basis is essential to keep up with the rate of the plant's development. Feed every 2 to 3 weeks with a general liquid garden fertilizer, or make your own if you choose. You should, of course, use a feed made specifically for houseplants. If the plant is overgrown and you don't want it any taller, stop fertilizing it and you want to encourage new growth.

REPOTTING

Young plants, the banana "pups," easily fill small pots, necessitating regular repotting into larger containers, perhaps twice or three times in the first year. At this stage, all you need is regular potting soil.

PROPAGATION

According to the Dwarf Cavendish's tendency for sucking, new "pups" will be born when the parent grows older. They can be gently taken away from

SCHLUMBERGERA GAERTNERI

(Easter Cactus)

The Easter cactus (also Rhipsalidopsis gaertneri) has a wide range of bloom colors. They're usually in bloom when you buy them, and they're popular holiday presents. Flowers come in a variety of colors, including white, crimson, green, peach, lavender, and pink.

The plant's peculiar appearance attracts the eye even after it has bloomed. New growth adds to the segments, giving them a rickety stacked feel. The plant lacks the spines of a desert cactus, instead taking on a more undulating shape with more pointing nodes on the leaf edges.

It has lovely knockout flowers that bloom in the months of March and April. When not in bloom, the Easter Cactus resembles the Christmas Cactus, and while both are relatively easy to care for and re-flower the following year, the Easter Cactus is less popular as a houseplant.

Easter Cactus Guide

LIGHT

Average lighting; don't expose it to heavy shadow or direct sunshine for extended periods of time. Deep shade produces no growth and few, if any, flowers. Since the Easter Cactus is not a desert cactus, it must be protected from direct sunshine. The leaves will turn reddish-brown if exposed to too much light.

WATERING

Like all cacti, they can store water in their thick fleshy leaves and survive droughts. However, if you leave the soil to dry out entirely for an extended period of time, the plant may begin to lose its leaf parts. Look for consistently damp rather than muddy soil, and use tepid rather than cool water when watering.

If the plant has been placed in a dry setting, placing the container in a pebble tray or misting the leaves a few times a month is advised (their natural habitat are shady, dank and moisture filled forests).

FEEDING

Feed once a month during the growing season with an all-purpose houseplant fertiliser.

TEMPERATURE

In most households, the average temperature is ideal for the Easter Cactus. From October to early the following year, the plant should be held in a slightly cooler (7°C - 15°C / 45°F - 59°F) climate. The most common option is an unheated space.

REPOTTING

It takes a long time for it to become pot bound because it grows slowly. If required, repot after flowering in early summer, but it's unlikely you'll need to do so more than once every few years.

SPEED OF GROWTH

During the growing season, slow but steady growth is to be expected.

HEIGHT/SPREAD

It's slow to rise, but it can stretch out over time and never get really tall.

ECHEVERIAS

Echeverias are pretty popular outdoors, but they've become very fashionable modern indoor houseplants in recent years. Despite their semi-desert origins in Central America, Mexico, and northwestern South America, they thrive as indoor plants. It's typical to see them grown in odd and visually arty pots and containers, much like many other small succulents. They're little houseplants, similar to the Haworthia, and they're always easy and quick to care for. You can go a month without watering them and they won't be too upset. However, to really make them shine, you must properly care for them.

The leaves come in a variety of shades, ranging from basic greens to more vibrant hues. These leaves usually develop a rosette pattern that stays with them throughout their whole existence.

The rosette shape allows for optimum light penetration while still allowing the plants to easily absorb and direct water down to the roots. Tehre are several reason why you may want an Echeveria in your house: first of all, it's hard to mess up with Echeverias so they make excellent plants for beginners. They make great presents and they are inexpensive (in truth, some of the rarer hybrids are expensive, but the more common types are really cheap to buy). Maintenance is easy and growth is slow even in ideal conditions, so that you may only need to repot it once every few years.

TRUST ME: *They are unique looking and frequently sold in stylish containers, they make super convenient birthday gifts that will leave a positive impression for years to come.*

Echeveria Care Guide

LIGHT

Almost all Echeveria plants thrive in bright, indirect sunlight. They struggle in low light and with persistent direct intense sunshine, especially if your watering skills aren't up to par.

Window ledges are ideal for your Echeveria, but if you want to keep one with a southern exposure, give it some shielding and move it as soon as you see any damage. Burned leaves do not heal, and since they expand slowly and retain their leaves for long periods, the burn can last a long time.

WATERING

Many succulents in the wild have evolved to heavy rains followed by a long period of time before the next one occurs. Many of their characteristics, such as their thick fleshy leaves and the way they funnel water directly to the roots, aid in this.

Echeverias appreciate a strong deep watering every now and then, followed by a wait before they dry out entirely or mostly. They aren't cacti, so they shouldn't be dehydrated for long periods of time. As a general rule, during the Spring and Summer, water deeply and often if the soil seems to be drying out. Water less deeply and wait until the soil dries out completely from late Fall to early Winter.

Watering them from above and through the middle of the plant is perfectly acceptable, even though many people would advise you not to. The primary explanation for this belief is that if water "sits" in the rosette it could remain there for hours, if not days, rotting the plant's central portion. Don't let your plant live in such conditions.

HUMIDITY

These are not tropical plants, despite being simple houseplants. Indoors, their biggest flaw is a lack of decent, consistent ventilation combined with extremely humid conditions. Such conditions will increase the likelihood of your plant rotting rapidly. Choose a spot that allows for some natural ventilation, such as near a window. However, attempting to cultivate it in a continuously steamy environment such as a bathroom or kitchen should be avoided.

TEMPERATURE

This kind of plant thrives in a warm environment. It'll handle the hottest rooms in your house with ease. On the other hand, if exposed to frosts or near sub-zero temperatures, they will actually fall apart and transform to mush overnight. To be healthy, we recommend never allowing the temperature to drop below 41°F (5°C).

REPOTTING AND SOIL

The Echeveria has a tendency to stretch out by producing offsets along the edges of the main plant. The adult plant can seldom outgrow its current container (unless you're beginning with a small, fast-growing plant), so if you want it to branch out and generate offsets, you'll need to consider repotting from time to time and make sure the container is larger than the previous one.

They don't require an especially deep container because they don't have a thick root systems. A too deep pot might raise the risk of accidental overwatering and eventual root rot. A shallow and big pot, rather than a deep and narrow one, is your best choice.

KALA CHOE BLOSSFELDIANA

(Flaming Katy)

Flaming Katy, Christmas Kalanchoe, Widow's Thrill, and Florist Kalanchoe are all common names for Kalanchoe Blossfeldiana. It is similar to the jade plant and belongs to the Crassulaceae tribe. Its genus contains over 125 tropical succulent species, the majority of which make excellent indoor plants.

Kalanchoe is a low-cost houseplant that, when in bloom, produces a stunning show of tiny but colorful flowers. The flowers, unfortunately, wilt soon. When this occurs, the plant's only offering is a small bouquet of succulent flowers, which some people may find unappealing.

TRUST ME: *It only needs to be watered when the soil is completely dry.*

Flaming Katy Care Guide

LIGHT

Kalanchoe can deal with dark places in your home - or workplace - for around one month. This means you can show off their beautiful, yet fleeting, flowers anywhere in your house.

In the long run. low light conditions will cause the plant to become leggy and spindly, destroying the compact structure of this houseplant. They need bright sunshine, preferably an hour or two of direct sunlight every day. If left without light for a prolonged time, it will inevitably die, and the flowers too. The plant can thrive if you choose areas with plenty of light.

WATERING

The Flaming Katy is ideal for the infrequent or forgetful indoor gardener, as it can withstand sporadic and sparse watering thanks to the succulent fleshy leaves' ability to store water for many weeks at a time.

When the soil has dried out somewhat, an attentive owner who wants a healthy plant will water heavily and then wait until it is dry again. This could be once a week during the summer. During the winter months, only a limited amount of water is needed every few weeks at most.

HUMIDITY

The humidity level isn't an issue with this succulent, as it is with many other succulents like houseplants. Even if your home's humidity is high, good ventilation will help avoid basal stem rot and fungus.

REPOTTING

If you decide to maintain the plant after it has stopped flowering, use a soil mix that is either very free draining or apply some grit or sand to the medium you are using while repotting. Repot after a couple of years but be vigilant since the leaves are very fragile and can break quickly if handled roughly.

SPEED OF GROWTH

Regardless of the conditions under which your plant is growing, it will do it slowly. However, since the plant is small to begin with, a little growth over the course of a season will also transform it. Between 3 and 5 years, the optimum height and spread are normally achieved.

HEIGHT / SPREAD

Indoor Kalanchoe rarely grow taller or wider than 12in/ 30cm, making for a delicate specimen. Use a compact vine for best looking results. If your plant gets leggy and spindly, you aren't giving them enough light.

SPATHIPHYLLUM

(Peace Lily)

Peace lilies are evergreen tropical plants that grow in dappled sunshine and consistent rainfall on the forest's floor. The trick to make your peace lily happy and safe is to replicate these circumstances at home. Peace lilies grow white to off-white flowers beginning in early summer and blooming throughout the year if given enough sun.

Peace lilies are a common option for offices and homes. When it comes to indoor plants, peace lily plants are among the simplest to maintain and one of the best to go with modern furniture.

Peace Lily Care Guide

LIGHT

The growth pf your plant would be faster and more vigorous if you place it in a bright spot without direct sunlight. Of course, if you want to cultivate it in a darkened region of your home, it will thrive, adapt, and grow, contrary to popular belief (albeit slowly).

WATERING

Keep the soil just moist at all times. Just keep an eye on the plant for visual cues when it's time to water. When the Lily feels good, you can see it right away, but when it wants water, it flops down. When watering, soak the plant rather than letting it "rest" in water. If you're having trouble with your lily, it's more likely because of how you're watering it.

HUMIDITY

If the humidity in these areas is consistently poor, it can create issues in the long run, so aim to raise the humidity in these areas. Otherwise, a light misting is all that's needed.

REPOTTING

If you do repot, do so in the spring if necessary, this will encourage flowering. You will just need a slightly larger pot and regular houseplant potting mix.

SPEED OF GROWTH

In decent lighting conditions, it will grow moderately. If light levels are low, it will be significantly slower (if at all).

HEIGHT / SPREAD

This is dependent on the kind of fruit you purchase. Even so, in an indoor home environment, they can only hope to grow to a height of 18in / 45cm.

HEDERA HELIX

(English Ivy)

English ivy, also known as Hedera Helix (from Ancient Greek, "twist or turn"), is a simple houseplant to cultivate. Plants of English ivy are evergreen perennials, and Woody vines are another name for them. English ivy should be used as a ground cover because it spreads horizontally and grows to a height of 8 inches. It is, however, a climber, thanks to its aerial rootlets, which allow it to reach heights up to 80 feet. While the plant can eventually produce small greenish flowers, it is mainly cultivated for its evergreen leaves, and in this respect it may be categorized as a foliage plant. Spring is the perfect season to grow English ivy. It's a fast-growing plant, so much that in some areas it is considered invasive.

Since English Ivy is not poisonous, it can be handled like any other herb. Its leaves though, as well as the berries produced by very mature specimens, can be poisonous if consumed.

English Ivy Care Guide

LIGHT

In general, English Ivy comes in variegated or all-green varieties. To keep its colors, the variegated version needs moderate to bright light. The all-green variety will thrive in darker environments, but its development will slow down as a result. However, no direct sunlight is suggested for any kind of ivy.

WATERING

Despite her origins in rainy England, English Ivy despises being soaked or bone dry. You can find a good balance by holding the soil moist. In winter, he soil stays wet for longer stretches of time, so won't need to water as much during the colder seasons.

HUMIDITY

If you want to place the plant in a hot room, you'll need to spray the leaves often, or find other means to keep level of humidity high.

REPOTTING

English Ivy takes a long time to fill a standard sized pot with its roots due to the work it takes to produce aerial roots along its winding stems. When it's time to repot (usually, every 2 to 3 years), you can do so at any time of the year with regular soil or simple potting compost.

SPEED OF GROWTH

Generally the Ivy's growth is quite aggressive. But direct sun will make it grow slower. If on the other hand you can find a comfy shaded spot and use fertilizer to encourage growing, growth can be fast paced, especially for two-year old and more plants.

HEIGHT/SPREAD

A mature Ivy can grow 9 feet per year and its branches will continue to thrive as long as they have enough to cling onto, or as long as you don't pinch out the tops.

JASMINUM POLYANTHUM

(Chinese / Star Jasmine)

Growing vining jasmines as houseplants can be challengeing, but one species that stands out for this purpose is pink jasmine (Jasminum polyathum), also known as white jasmine, Chinese jasmine, or winter-blooming jasmine. White jasmine blooms in late winter, with a profusion of reddish-pink buds that open to reveal star-shaped white flowers tinged with pink. It's rare for houseplants to flower too profusely. Growing jasmine it's ideal for your house if a soft night-time scent, spread by its winter blooms, appeal to your senses.

Although not all jasmine flowers are scented, Jasminum polyanthum, the variety most commonly grown indoors, has a sweet aroma that is especially fragrant at night.

Star Jasmine Care Guide

LIGHT

Both Jasmine plants, whether grown outdoors or indoors, need bright light and, if possible, direct sunlight, so a south-facing window would be ideal for your plant.

WATERING

A Jasmine would need a lot of water when it is in bloom and growing. When in bloom it's very important to remember that the soil must be kept moist nearly all the time. If the soil dries up, the flowers and buds that are about to bloom will wither. Always remember though that with the term "moist" I don't mean soggy or for the plant to sit in a tray of water, that is more on the "wet" side, not "moist", they're not equivalent.

REPOTTING

You're going to need to repot when the Jasmine outgrows its pot. Repotting into larger pots on a regular basis encourages growing, so you can only repot when the roots have fully filled the pot. The best time to do this is in the spring or summer but do not do repot when the buds are already growing. The best compost mix is a standard compost mix that drains well.

SPEED OF GROWTH

During the warmer months of the year, the growth rate of Jasmine can best be characterized as robust. Otherwise, the plant will clamber and ascend, resulting in a messy appearance (if you're okay with that, then let it grow freely).

CRASSULA OVATA

(Jade Plant / Money Plant)

The legend says that there is a plant that is able to bring you wealth and prosperity. If you were wondering what is that plant, it's the beautiful jade plant!

The Jade plant is commonly known as the Money Plant, and together with the Pachira Aquatica, is the most popular "lucky charm plants". The Jade Plant is one of the most well-known (and loved) of the various succulent Crassula used as indoor plants.

The Feng Shui money plants' energy comes from their deep roots and vivid energy of the developing young plant. It is said that you should place her somewhere which somehow represent your finances or your bank account for it to work (for example the table or the drawer where you always use to place your wallet).

Jade Plant Care Guide

LIGHT

A location with a lot of natural sunlight doesn't mean that it will not survive in marginally darker environments... actually it can also thrive in a space with no windows but with artificial lighting!

The leaves can turn a dark purple color if the sunlight is too harsh or the plant is not used to it. If this your case, either place it to a slightly darker place or make more light hit the plant gradually, over time. After few weeks, the purple should disappear and return to the familiar lime green.

WATERING

Jade Plants, like most succulents, are tough and adaptable to a range of conditions, but they won't last long if you overwater them all the time. Water thoroughly and wait for the soil to dry before repeating. In the winter, only enough water should be provided to keep the soil moist.

REPOTTING

Several Crassula species, like the Jade, are happy to remain in the same pot and stale soil for years on end. They don't need to be repotted as much, which is a major plus for an house plant. These plants get big and strong!

When repotting, do it in the spring and be extra vigilant about watering before new fresh growth appears. You'll need a compost blend that drains well.

SPEED OF GROWTH

In the early years, you should assume sluggish to moderate development in good light conditions with a consistent watering schedule. After it reaches maturity, its growth will be a bit more lazy.

HEIGHT/SPEED

The Jade Plant is incredible. It will comfortably equal the average human life span and grow up to a height of 12ft / 4m during that period. It can stretch to over 3ft in diameter, so plenty of room is needed if you want it for the long term. If you have a tiny one, though, don't worry; it will take a long time for it to hit these proportions. And who knows, by the time it requires more rooms, it might have boosted your bank account, paid off your mortgage, and allowed you to purchase a larger home to accommodate it!

TRUST ME: Jewel Orchids are cultivated for their dark foliage rather than their exotic flowers.

JEWEL ORCHID

(Ludisia Discolour)

Ludisia discolour, also known as the "Jewel Orchid," is a satisfying and simple-to-care-for houseplant. Its deep purple leaves are flecked with pink streaks and have a velvety look, tolerant of lower light and fond of humidity. Tiny white flowers emerge among the leaves in the right circumstances, rendering this plant a treat for a shadier corner.

The Jewel Orchid (Ludisia discolour) is a unique orchid with stunning dark, ovate-shaped leaves with pink veins. Jewel orchids produce whitish flowers on long flower spikes only once a year. Jewel orchids, unlike many other orchid plants, grow in the ground and enjoy the shade. and

Jewel Orchid Care Guide

LIGHT

The Jewel Orchid grows low in the ground in its natural habitat, sometimes in sunny areas. If you want to obtain the best results, place it under direct sunshine in your home or workplace.

North-facing rooms are ideal, but also any other positioning would work as long as the leaves are shielded from any harsh sunshine that might filter in during the day. Do not mistake this for a plant that thrives in the dark; heavy gloom should be avoided almost as well as bright sunshine if you want your plant to thrive.

WATERING

The Jewel Orchid prefers to flourish in mildly moist conditions. It doesn't like bone dry soil, but it also doesn't like dripping wet soil; if its roots are submerged in water, it will quickly perish.

Water the plant thoroughly, and wait until it is completely dried before watering it again. Wait until the top inch is dry before adding more water, as a general rule. You'll need to spray more often if you're using a more porous potting mix than if you're using regular potting soil so it can dry out faster.

HUMIDITY

Humidity is not a big deal if you got the watering conditions just right. If you know you're a slacker when it comes to watering, help your Jewel Orchid out by growing the humidity in theroom. This would provide a little hedge for your plant to compensate for the lack of watering.

For my experience this plant is perfect for flourishing in bottle gardens, but if you want it to bloom, don't bother: the blooms spoil rapidly in the extremely damp conditions created by the bottle where the plant is kept.

FEEDING

Jewel's orchids are not that hungry, and you'll be fine if you just feed your plant a few times per year. It doesn't matter whether you use a specialty orchid feed or anything more generic; it's not picky, and it will work.

REPOTTING

When the pot becomes overcrowded or the plant becomes wobbly and top-heavy, repot it. Since the roots of these orchids stretch out rather than grow tall, they don't need a deep container. Instead, you might use a shallow and big pot.

Unlike certain orchids, you should use regular potting soil, but you must pay attention to the plant's watering needs to prevent overwatering. Normal potting soil is intended to retain water, but if you unintentionally saturate it, the water can remain in the soil for a long time, greatly increasing the risk of rotting.

SPREADH /WIDTH

Since these orchids like to stretch rather than grow tall, they are often larger than they are tall. The flowering stem will almost triple or double the plant's height.

MONSTERA DELICIOSA

(Swiss Cheese Plant)

This one is everybody's favorite. Probably the queen of houseplants! If you're looking for a plant that resembles a modern art masterpiece, well look no further, you've found it. You've probably already seen her on an interior design magazine, or on somebody'd social media feed, but If you have a room corner that needs to be "arted up" a notch, make sure to grab one of those. These tropical plants can grow up to 10 feet tall and have leaves as large as 12 inches in diameter!

The Swiss cheese plant gets its name from its large, heart-shaped leaves that host holes (called "fenestration") as the plant ages, giving it the appearance of Swiss cheese. The "Delicious Monster" is a tropical annual that is commonly cultivated which is native to Central and South America. It's known for being easy to care for and for her climbing qualities, so supplying it with a stake, moss stick, or trellis to cling to will result in some stunning displays (plus, it will produce larger leaves).

Swiss Cheese Plant Care Guide

LIGHT

Because of their tropical roots, Swiss cheese plants thrive in bright, indirect light or partial shade. They're used to grow in the jungle under the shade of big trees, and they can quickly get burned if exposed to too much direct sunlight. If direct sunshine is inevitable, limit their morning sun exposure to only two or three hours.

Swiss cheese plants like their watering to be regular and on the moist side, but not soaked. Although striking the balance can seem quite difficult, you can quickly determine whether your plant requires water by sticking your finger into the soil about an inch deep before watering your Monstera plant; if the soil seems almost dry to the touch, it's time to water.

TEMPERATURE AND HUMIDITY

The most popular Swiss cheese plants are always grown in a conservatory or greenhouse setting, as these deep-jungle plants rely on high humidity, plenty of moisture, and high temperatures. The more closely you can recreate the plant's natural environment, the better. Mist the plant regularly and place it in a well-lit, wet, and humid bathroom or kitchen. Additionally, a humidifier could also be used nearby to keep the air moist. If unavoidable, you can keep the Monstera above 60 degrees Fahrenheit for a short amount of time, but expect it to experience some die-back.

REPOTTING

Shortly after purchase, a young plant in its first container would need to be repotted. Find a pot that is somewhat larger than the old one, and pot it up into its new home using new compost, as with other houseplants. For at least three months, don't feed (with fertilize) freshly repotted plants.

IS THE MONSTERA DELICIOSA TOXIC?

Watch out for your pets: unfortunately, small animals such as dogs and cats may be poisoned by the Swiss cheese plant. The problem stems from the presence of insoluble calcium oxalate crystals in the plant's leaves, stems, and roots. Even though the Swiss cheese plant is rarely lethal, it's still necessary to call a veterinarian or other medical providers if your pet exhibits any unusual symptoms.

PHALAENOPSIS

(Moth Orchid)

Colorful, long-lasting, and easy to cultivate, the moth orchid is the perfect flower.

The Moth Orchid, also known as the Phalaenopsis Orchid or Phal's, is a well-known and quickly recognizable houseplant. They don't need much maintenance and can last for months on end. They've arguably done more than any other genus to increasing orchids' popularity in general.

Orchids of the genus Phalaenopsis are a very satisfying plant for the eye. They're not fussy, and under the right circumstances, they'll put on a show for months.

Moth Orchid Care Guide

LIGHT

Orchids that thrive in bright, indirect light are known as Light Orchids. The best quality of light comes from an east-facing window. Western or southern light is good as long as it's indirect. North-facing windows don't have adequate illumination in most cases.

WATERING

Overwatering rather than underwatering is more likely to consume a moth orchid (Phalaenopsis sp. and its hybrids). Orchids are commonly grown in bark or sphagnum moss, all of which must be left to dry between watering. (Because bark retains less water than moss, orchids planted in it need more frequent watering.) Water the orchid thoroughly until the bark or moss is dried to the touch and the container is lighter (until water comes through the drainage hole in the bottom of your pot). Orchid roots can never be left in stagnant water. Miniature moth orchids, which are relatively new to the market, are cultivated in smaller pots and can dry out more quickly.

REBLOOMING

You should cut off the bloom spike at the base of an orchid until it has finished flowering. Continue to fertilize. Place the pot in clear, bright light. Within a year, the orchid should flower again.

REPOTTING

The orchid may need to be repotted every few years. Since repotting an orchid will stress it and cause it to lose its blooms, do it while it isn't blooming.

CHRYSANTHEMUM MORIFOLIUM

(Pot Mum / Florist's Mum)

Tall, elegant flowers crown a mass of dark-green foliage on the Florist Chrysanthemum. This vine, including daisies, sunflowers, and marigolds, belongs to the Asteraceae family.

The name Chrysanthemum comes from the Greek words chryos, which means gold, and anthemom, which means herb. These "golden roses" come in a variety of colors, including pink, black, crimson, burgundy, white, and, of course, golden yellow.

The Pot Mum, also known as the Florist's Mum, is a common houseplant that is often given as a gift at Christmas, Easter, or Mothering Sunday. It is granted to an individual as a sign of motherhood in certain parts of the world, such as shortly after the recipient has given birth.

Pot Mum Care Guide

LIGHT

Bright light is needed in all situations. The weak winter sun, or early morning / late afternoon Summer sun will be most beneficial.

WATERING

Watering the Pot Mum leads to a high transpiration rate, which is one of the reasons it is so good at cleaning the air. For best result, you will need to water it often, perhaps twice a week. Maintain constant moisture in the soil.

HUMIDITY

There is no reason to be careful with humidity if the plant is being used as a temporary pot plant. If you want to keep it for a long time, keep it away from very dry and low-humidity environments.

FEEDING

Any decent all-purpose fertilizer once a month.

REPOTTING

Repotting isn't necessary because it won't be around long enough to outgrow it. The Crysnthemus container it comes in. If you plan on having it, follow standard repotting procedures. i.e., replace the current pot with a slightly larger one.

Flowers are usually the prime justification for purchasing a plant in the first place. While the doubles look good with their upbeat cheerleader pompon like appearance, the single flowers with the daisy like yellow centers are the most common. Except for blue and black, they are available in any color hue.

EFFICIENT AIR CLEANERS

Beautiful florist chrysanthemums work hard at reducing air pollution present in homes caused by contaminants in upholstery, paint, and carpet, including being transient houseguests. "Florist mums are one of the safest flowering plants for removing formaldehyde, benzene, and ammonia from indoor air".

EPIPREMNUM AUREUM

(Pothos / Devil's Ivy / Scindapsus)

Pothos, one of the most popular plant in the houseplant realm. Also known as Devil's Ivy, is a low-maintenance houseplant that is almost foolproof to cultivate indoors. It can be seen in people's houses, offices, and even shopping malls. When you start to notice, it's everywhere!

Because of its beautiful light lime-colored leaves with yellow variegation, golden pothos is one of the most common varieties of hanging basket plants. The lemon-colored brush strokes on its leaves together with their sinuous shapes makes it also very elegant. The pothos helps br shaded corners with its shiny leaves.

The golden pothos is an exceptional low-light herb, which is one (notable characteristics. Plants with variegated leaves typically vibrancy when exposed to low light; the golden pothos, on the ot keeps its vivid variegation even in low light. Because of this, gold is a good choice for a bedroom plant with access to minimal ligh

TRUST ME: *These vines are very easy to care for and can gr a variety of lighting and watering conditions.*

Pothos Care Guide

LIGHT

If you chose a very dark place, growth will be gradual, and the "vines" will be thin, with leaves spaced far apart. Very bright patches of direct sunshine on the leaves should also be avoided, as this would inevitably kill the plant. If the room is so bright that you have to squint your eyes to be able to read a book, it is probably a room where your Pothos would be unhappy to live. Despite their hardiness, too much sun will cause their leaves to yellow and 'burn,' so keep them away from the windowsill.

WATERING

Areate the soil in your pot if you have a new plant. Before watering check there is no moist 1 inch under the soil's surface. During winters water more sparingly. The Pothos is drought tolerant, so your plant won't mind too much if sometimes you delay the watering. Overwatering, on the other hand, must be prevented at all costs, or rot will develop around the roots. It is never a good idea to have soggy or muddy soil. Pour some extra water away if you've supplied too many.

A decent soak once a week is probably best. Many factors, however are in play: plants in warm rooms with loads of light require more water than those in colder spots with less light.

REPOTTING

It will take some years for the Pothos to need repotting. The most noticeable indication that it's time for a repot is when it is no longer expanding in sum mer time (growth shouldn't be expected in the winter).

Pothos like to stretch their muscles out as well. If your vines get long and twisted, gently hang their branches on a few tacked pins around their growing space and you'll have lovely vines growing around your walls in no time.

OXALIS

(Purple Shamrock / False or Love Plant)

This one will probably not appeal everybody, but I find its beauty one of the most fascinating plant that can be kept inside our house. Get one of this and you can be consider a houseplant pro.

With its purple foliage - sometimes nearly black - the Purple shamrock (Oxalis triangularis), also known as false shamrock, will unavoidably draw the interest of the whole room they're placed in. Its deep purple leaves are triangular in shape and usually emerge in threes. The way the leaves of these plants close at night is a curious touch. In the evening, the leaves fold down like an umbrella, and remain closed during the night (or on especially cloudy days), but they open up again with the morning sun.

Other rare responsive houseplants have identical movements (Mimosa pudica).

The plant produces tiny flowers that range in color from white to pale pink or lavender. Purple shamrock thrives as a houseplant and is better grown in the spring.

Purple Shamrock Care Guide

LIGHT

This plant thrives under a wide range of conditions, from full sun to partial shade. If you're raising it outside in a hot environment, give it some shade from the sun during the afternoon. The plant should be grown near a window that receives plenty of light. Rotate the pot on a regular basis to ensure that both sides of the plant are exposed to light and are rising uniformly. The plant will become sluggish and leggy if it receives insufficient light.

SOIL

Purple shamrocks can thrive in a variety of soil types as long as they have adequate drainage. If the soil absorbs so much moisture, the roots are vulnerable to rotting. The perfect soil is loamy or sandy. A general, well-draining potting mix should suffice for container development.

WATERING

Water to ensure an even amount of soil moisture, especially for young purple shamrock plants. More mature plants are drought tolerant and will forgive the occasionale lack of watering. Feed purple shamrock plants once the top inch of soil has dried out during the growing season. In the summer, when the plant is dormant, water it gently every two to three weeks to keep the soil from drying out entirely.

TEMPERATURE AND HUMIDITY

These plants prefer temperatures between 60 to 75 degrees Fahrenheit, making them ideal for growing indoors in typical room temperatures. They can withstand temperatures as low as 50 degrees Fahrenheit at night. Protect the plants from strong winds, including those from air conditioners and heaters, which can harm the foliage. Purple shamrock plants thrive in a moderately humid environment.

FERTILIZER

During the growing season, fertilize the purple shamrock plant with a slow-release or liquid fertilizer. A liquid fertilizer for houseplants is suitable for indoors use. Incorporating compost into the soil will also aid in the promotion of healthy development.

IS THE PURPLE SHAMROCK TOXIC?

When swallowed, oxalis plants are poisonous to both humans and animals. Both areas of the plant are toxic, with the bulbs having the largest concentration of toxins.

CHLOROPHYTUM

(Spider Plant)

Spider plants (or Chlorophytum comosum) have a rosette of long, thin, arched foliage that is either solid green or white variegated. These houseplants are particularly attractive in a hanging basket and were common in Victorian-era homes.

TRUST ME: When the flowers fade, tiny plantlets appear in their place, eventually growing their own seeds.

Spider plants are among the most common houseplants to cultivate, despite their creepy-crawly name. They can thrive in less-than-ideal environments, and they look beautiful when grown in a tropical environment. The leaves of these plants are slender and softly arching, ranging in length from 1 to 1.5 feet on average. The leaves may be grey or green and white striped. Long stems with tiny star-shaped flowers are frequently sent out by mature plants.

Spider Plant Care Guide

LIGHT

To retain their stripes, all variegated Spider Plants need a bright spot. The all-green version (which has no variegation to lose) can evolve in a darker setting, but at a much slower rate. Direct sunlight should be avoided at all costs.

WATERING

In the growing months (Spring to Autumn/Fall), water your plant thoroughly, and if you've placed it in a bright spot, you'll see rapid growth and a fair chance of Spider babies. Water sparingly in the winter because growth slows down regardless of what you do, and too much water sloshing around the roots will cause the plant to rot.

REPOTTING

If given proper care, a Spider Plant would need to be repotted into a larger pot every Spring before it reaches maturity, which takes around 2 to 5 years. You may use standard houseplant or garden compost for this. If you're concerned that your plant is already too big and you won't be able to move it, don't repot it into a larger jar, as this will limit its growth.

HOYA KERRII

(Sweetheart Plant / Valentine Hoya)

There are a few Hoya species that make excellent houseplants, one of which is Hoya kerrii, also known as the Sweetheart Vine. While it has grown in popularity in recent years, you might still have trouble finding facts or care tips regarding this plant. If you think the leaves of Hoya kerrii are the cutest thing about it, just wait after it blooms. The flowers have a strong scent, making them a good source of perfume fragrances.

Hoya Kerrii Care Guide

LIGHT

This plant would need a moderate amount of light to thrive, but it will survive in a shadier area too. However, very dark areas should be avoided. Sunlight is also appropriate, because it may be placed virtually anywhere in your home or workplace.

WATERING

The Hoya can store water for long stretches of time between waterings thanks to its succulent qualities. For the most part, this makes it a hardy and low-maintenance plant; however, if this is the only treatment you will be willing to give her, do not expect much love back. Water it regularly when the soil has dried out and you can hope for them to reward you with one of the most beautiful and peculiar flower houseplants could give you. As always, be careful not to go overboard! The soil should never be wet or flooded, since this would bring rot. Take extra precautions, especially if the pot you're using doesn't have any drainage holes.

FEEDING

Because the plant only has one leaf, only a small amount of fertilizer is needed, twice a year. You can feed it a little more if you have an older plant or if the single leaf is producing new shoots. If that's the case, I suggest to not doing it more than four times a year.

REPOTTING

This topic is a source of controversy among Hoya owners. There are many schools of thinking that can be boiled down to the following "rules":

- The soil mix must drain well and not have a lot of rich organic matter.
- Plants that are root or pot attached in small containers are more likely to bloom (this only applies to mature plants with many leaves).
- No matter how big or old the plant is, if the pot is too little, it will not mature.
- A large pot for plants with just one leaf has a much higher chance of rotting due to unintended overwatering (so don't do it).

So, to put it all into perspective, here are few explanations that should make sense:

- Young plants with only one leaf can be repotted only as new growth appears.

- Young plants with a few leaves can be repotted every couple of years, each time going up into a much larger tank.
- Mature plants with several leaves can be repotted every couple of years at the maximum, each time going up into a slightly larger container.

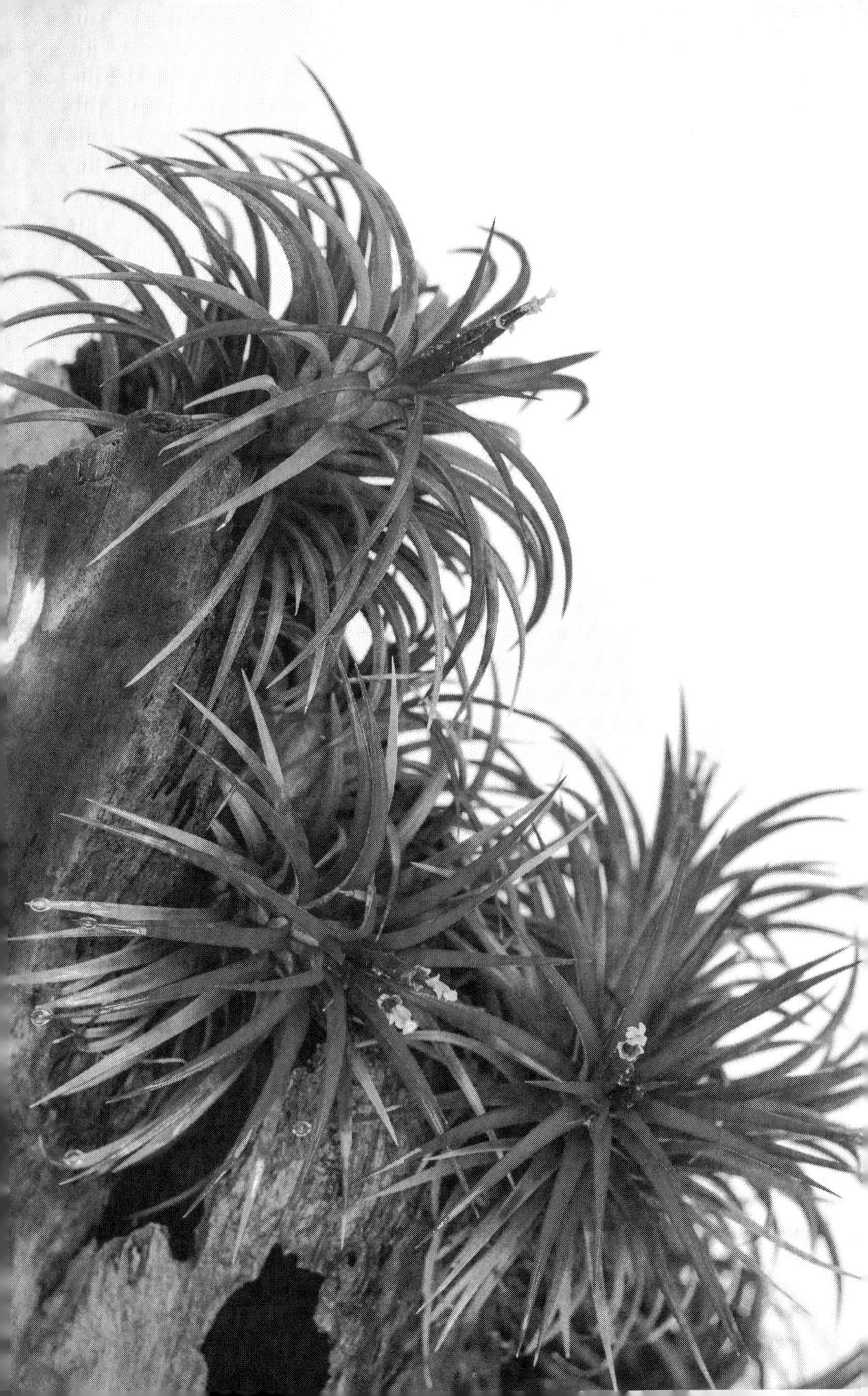

TILLANDSIA

(Blue Flowered Torch)

Tillandsia cyanea, or Pink Quill Plant, is a lovely little plant. This plant is one of the most common and simplest to grow bromeliads, and it can be used as a small container plant, hanging basket, or epiphyte attached to wood.

The blue-flowered torch is a perennial herb that grows on a variety of plants. It has 30 to 50 cm rosettes of arching dark green leaves. Green to purple-pink floral bracts and funnel-shaped, scented white-eyed, deep purple-blue flowers with spreading petals are produced by this herb. The flower-flowering stem is a plump blade-like feather that can reach 7,8 inches in length and is made up of thick, flattened pink bracts from which the large, bluish flowers emerge, often referred to by bromeliad collectors as a "paddle-shaped inflorescence."

Tillandsa Care Guide

LIGHT

The perfect light for your Pink Quill Plant is clear, natural light. That's where an east or west exposure comes in handy. You want it in this light to encourage flowering and keep the plant satisfied over time. Do not put the Tillandsia under direct sunlight, not the right kind of light for this little tender beauty.

WATERING

Very low effort is needed to maintain the Tillandsia in good shape. Water it once or max twice a week, depending on how dusty the conditions are.

Water less in the late fall/winter months, as with all houseplants. If the water is rough, use purified or distilled water instead, as this plant is sensitive to mineral build-up in tap water. Some prefer to use tap water that has sat long enough for the chlorine contained to dissipate. Try and see to what kind of water your plant react better.

FERTILIZING

I rarely fertilize my bromeliads or air plants; only once a year if they seem to need it. This plant gets its moisture and nutrients from the leaves rather than the soil, for this reason, it's best to spray the fertilizer onto the foliage & the surface of the growing medium.

You may use this fertilizer designed for air plants or an all-purpose orchid food diluted to 1/2 strength. You can fertilize in the spring and/or summer, and it should be done once or twice a year.

REPOTTING

If you buy a Tillandsia that is already in bloom, there is no need to repot it. Repot and upsize the pot next spring if the roots have filled the pot and/or you see a young offset.

Don't worry if this doesn't happen because the Pink Quill plant's roots are simple and compact. It's important to always be aware if there is at least a tiny amount of room for new roots to expand through. The potting mix you select must be free drainage, which means regular potting compost combined with a little grit or perlite would suffice.

AECHMEA FASCIATA

(Urn Plant / Silver Vase plant)

Aechmea fasciata is a flowering bromeliad plant that can be cultivated both indoors and outdoors, depending on the environment. The Urn plant has a completely different impact if you observe it from far rather than you do it by a closer inspection.

The urn bulb is one the most common Aechmea genus bromeliad for growing and displaying indoors. The traditional name come from the fact that the plant's core resembles an urn or vase. This vase form captures water in its natural environment, and the grower should fill it as much as nature expected. After a couple of years of maturity, this plant develops a large flower head that can last from mid-summer to early winter.

When an Aechmea Fasciata reaches maturity (after a few years), it produces a bract that becomes bright pink over time. It has a long flowering cycle, and these plants truly reward their owners with the familiar, long-lasting inflorescence during this time.

Urn Plant Care Guide

LIGHT

The majority of Bromeliads are epiphytic, meaning they grow on larger plants such as trees. Visualize a plant catching on a tree trunk so you can imagine how it will flourish in its natural habitat. In this environment, her natural home is below the canopy and away from the harsh direct light, away from the very dark sunny spots at the base of the tree.

When growing these plants in our homes, attempt to provide bright indirect light to imitate their preferred light conditions. It can also thrive in light shade but avoid heavy shade or rooms with no curtains.

If you want to get the plant to flowering level, you'll need more sun. Avoid direct sunshine at all costs, or you risk scorching the leaves and forever destroying the plant's aspect.

WATERING

Aechmea are opportunistic plants in their natural habitat, collecting water in their central "vase" or "urns." The flower bract arises from the vase, which is the central container. They don't have a large root system, but the majority of their irrigation needs are fulfilled by the water contained in their urns. Since these houseplants aren't big drinkers, don't overwater them at any point. Keep the central vase full, emptying and refilling it once a month to keep the liquid from being stagnant.

If the vase is full, you just need to water the compost until it dries out entirely. This will most likely happen every few weeks. And even more so in very hot weather. If you don't want to water with a vase, try to keep the soil partially damp at all times.

TEMPERATURE

If given the choice, all Aechmea would prefer warmer temperatures. However, they aren't too concerned about temperature in general. Temperatures range from 59°F (15°C) to 77°F (25°C).

TRADESCANTIA ZEBRINA

(Wandering Jew Plant / Inch Plant)

The Wandering Jew, also known as the Inch Rose, Spiderwort, or Tradescantia Zebrina, is a houseplant that can be grown in a hanging basket to display its long trailing vines or kept enclosed and compact in a pot. This plant is very flexible, quick to grow, and difficult to destroy, making it an excellent indoor plant to have around.

As a hanging or trailing indoor vine, Tradescantia zebrina is valued for its ease of care and colorful foliage of silver, purple, and green that brightens up any room.

TRUST ME: *Wandering Jew (or, more recently, Wandering Dude) gets its name from its ability to effectively root and survive in a variety of environments.*

Wandering Jew Plant Care Guide

LIGHT

The variegated colors on the leaves of all Tradescantias, including the Wandering Jew Plants, require a lot of light to stay vibrant; if the light is too dark, the colors will fade.

In the other hand, if it is exposed to too much illumination, leaf scorching occurs; luckily, however, the phenomenon of "too much light" is mostly exacerbated by overly exposed areas during the season. This is difficult to do indoors, so you'll only be at risk if you let your plants outside in Summer.

WATERING

As you'd imagine from any hardy houseplant, the Wandering Jew can handle droughts and a little water logging now and again.

However, if that's how you water your plants you should stop this sloppy watering technique as soon as possible: if you want a good-looking plant, it needs to be properly watered. The method is simple: water your Tradescantia often and liberally during the summer months to keep the soil moist for as long as possible. In the winter, cut back sharply so development can stall or cease entirely, reducing the need for water drastically.

REPOTTING

It's best to repot once a year to allow the roots a little more room to flourish, but this plant, like many houseplant, will survive growing in the same soil for years. This is especially useful if you've wanted to grow it in a hanging basket, which can be fiddly to upsize and difficult to deal with.

When you do need to repot, regular potting soil is a perfect option; just quit the mixes with a lot of manure and don't use ordinary dirt from your yard.

ZAMIOCULCAS ZAMIIFOLIA

(ZZ Plant)

Zamioculcas zamiifolia, also known as the ZZ plant, is a tropical perennial native to Eastern Africa that has gained worldwide popularity in recent years due to its adaptability to a variety of conditions. The soft, naturally glossy leaves of the ZZ vary in color from light lime in youth, to emerald green in maturity.

With its large, beautiful, dark green leaves, the ZZ plant has a lot of advantages for offices and homes. The ZZ plant is tolerant of neglect, drought, and low light levels without being too much irritated. The waxy leaves reflect light and can brighten rooms. ZZ grows slowly to a height and width of two to three feet, which means this isn't a monster plant that easily outgrows containers.

The ZZ Plant has a number of advantages, including being trendy, beautiful, and easy to care for, as well as having a simple propagation process.

ZZ Plant Care Guide

LIGHT

This plant thrives in medium to poor indirect sunlight. Allows for bright indirect light to be used. Intense, direct sunlight is not recommended.

Early morning or late afternoon sun is preferable, so choose a window that faces north, east, or west. If you want it to flourish, you should also keep it out of deep shade.

WATERING

Enable 2-3 weeks between waterings to allow the soil to dry out. Watering should be done more often in higher light and less often in lower light.

Since the plant is adapted to surviving droughts, frequent watering without allowing the soil to dry between applications will make the leaves yellow before rotting the tubers.

The soil, on the other hand, needs to be damp for the majority of the time between late Spring and early Autumn / Fall for productive and rapid development.

HUMIDITY

Average home humidity is fine; dry air can be tolerated.

TEMPERATURE

Temperatures range from 60°F to 85°F. The average temperature of our houses will most likely make the ZZ's life more than comfortable.

SIZE

The ZZ may grow slowly, but at the peak of its growth it can reach a height between 16" to 28".

IS THE ZAMIOCULCAS ZAMIIFOLIA TOXIC?

Yes, when swallowed, it is poisonous. But by now you should have realized that houseplants should be kept out of sight of young children and pets anyway.

CYCLAMEN PERSICUM

(Cyclamen)

Cyclamen (Cyclamen persicum) is a compact flowering plant with sweet-scented, small (1/2- to 3/4-inch) blooms on long stems rising above the foliage. The Cyclamen is a tuberous annual, which means it dies down to its dense roots (tubers) in the summer and regrows easily in the fall. Its flowers are pink, yellow, red, and white in color. It also has medium-green heart-shaped leaves with silver marbling.

It's widely grown as a houseplant, and it's especially popular during the holidays, when you can find cyclamen blooming on store shelves.
Indoors, cyclamens are normally cultivated in pots. They go dormant during the summer, but given a decent treatment, it can rebloom in the fall.

TRUST ME: *The timing of cyclamen's full dormancy is determined by its rising conditions.*

Cyclamen Care Guide

SOIL

Cyclamen favors a mildly acidic soil pH and organically rich, well-draining soil. You may use standard potting mix for container plants but add some sphagnum peat to the soil to increase the acidity.

WATERING

The presence of leaves indicates that the plant is actively growing. Water if the soil feels dry about an inch below the surface. Water should not be applied to the plant's leaves or crown (the area where the stem joins the roots), since this will most likely cause it to rot. Water infrequently when the plant is inactive (losing any or more of its leaves), just enough to keep the soil from drying out completely.

TEMPERATURE AND HUMIDITY

Cyclamen plants dislike high temperatures, draughts, and dry air. They thrive in a climate that is similar to their natural habitat, with temperatures ranging from 40 to 50 degrees Fahrenheit at night and 60 to 70 degrees Fahrenheit during the day. The importance of high humidity, particularly in the winter, cannot be overstated. Hold the plant on a tray filled with water and pebbles to increase humidity, just make sure the pot is not in contact with the water (as this could cause root rot).

Usually this plant stays outside; if you do bring your plant back inside if the weather gets cold. A safe rule of thumb is to put it indoors when the weather is already pleasant enough to open the curtains.

FERTILIZER

When in full leaf, feed your cyclamen plant with a diluted liquid low-nitrogen fertilizer every couple of weeks.

CHAPTER 3
The World of Succulent

WHAT ARE SUCCULENT PLANTS?

Succulents are water-storing plants with fleshy, thickened leaves and/or bloated roots. The word "succulent" is derived from the Latin word sucus, which means "juice or sap". Succulents are very drought resistant and they can thrive on small water supply such as dew and mist. For this reason they are ideal for new aspiring houseplant growers.

Succulents come in a wide variety of varieties and cultivars, spanning many plant families, but most people equate succulents with the cactus genus, Cactaceae. (Keep in mind, however, that although cacti are succulents, succulents are not all cacti).

Based on personal experience, my suggestion is: never underestimated the power of a succulent in a living room. They've been used in interior decor magazines, and on social media, as part of lavish wedding centrepieces, but also in minimalistic environments, where they give the focal point that enriches the room.

Right now, succulents are quite the trend. The oft-repeated assertion that succulents are simple to grow is only partially true. I'm going to give you some guidelines to follow if you want to successfully host succulents or cacti in your home.

Having said that, if you mess this up, you're good at messing things up.

WHAT SUCCULENTS NEED:

1. The right amount of light

The most complex environmental element to replicate indoors is the ambient light in a plant's native habitat. This aspect is easier to deal with when growing traditional houseplants. Many of them are used to the alternating cycles of shade and sun that occur in your household, having grown up in tropical jungles. After all, that's what happens as the sun rays pass through a tree canopy.

You're begging for disappointment if you put a plant that's used to being out in the scorching sun for a full 12 hours on an east-facing sill.

Choose the sunniest south-facing window you can find, and if none of your windows face south, go with a more tolerant succulent like aloe or give up and go get a sturdy Pothos.

2. The right amount of water

The Chihuahuan Desert receives just over 9 inches of rain a year, a drop in the bucket as opposed to the lush deserts that most of us call home. When it rains in the desert, though, it pours. To keep your desert-dwelling pet comfortable, attempt to imitate the rain patterns seen in its natural environment. Turn on the taps and let loose a deluge on your cacti instead of a trickle. Succulents (and all plants, for that matter) profit from a thorough soaking, which can last until the water runs out from the bottom of the container. Wait until the soil is fully dried before watering succulents again. Succulent's dislike sitting in wet dirt, so irrigation is important to avoid rot. A drainage hole should be present in your container to allow excess water to drain. Beginners can use terra-cotta pots.

3. The right Potting Soil

From ferns to fiddle-leaf figs, most potted plants come in a standard soil mix that fits with almost any kind of plant. The issue: succulents are designed to survive one of the harshest conditions on the planet, so regular potting soil won't suffice.

Adjust the soil in your succulent baby's home to a desert-dweller blend, which consists of half potting soil and something inorganic like perlite. Most succulents can thrive in this super well-draining, low-nutrient soil, whether they're used to thriving in the high and dry Andes or the scorching bottom lands of Death Valley.

4. The right amount of space

One big blunder is overcrowding succulents. Succulents are always packaged in cute little bowls, stuffed cheek to jowl. This set up is not the best idea though, as they are among the plants that don't like this setup. It is actually one of the most effective ways to promote mold and insect infestations.

The second problem is that, while succulents can survive on very little, they do need food and water. It is possible they start to suffer if there's so much competition. If your succulents arrive in a crowded arrangement, carefully separate them and give each one its own mini desert dune.

5. Grow the right Types

I know it's difficult to fight the temptation to cultivate saguaros (your typical desert cactus) indoors, but please don't. Some wild things, no matter how lovely their flowers or alluring their shape, are simply not meant to be tamed. Instead, go for the tough little cookies that will gladly embrace the windowsill as their forever home.

If you're dealing in indoor environments, Crassula and Sansevieria (a.k.a. snake plant) are fine choices. If you're searching for a prickly plant friend, the Mammillaria cacti (named after their woolly hair) is a fine option.

6. Get Rid of Bugs

Indoor succulents may be pest-free, but you will have to deal with pests on occasion. Gnats are drawn to succulents that have been planted in wet soils with poor drainage. Spray the soil with 70% isopropyl alcohol to get rid of eggs and larvae. Another insect that succulent owners must contend with is mealybugs. Mealybugs are commonly caused by overwatering and overfertilizing. Spray contaminated plants with 70% isopropyl alcohol and move them away from other succulents.

IDENTIFYING YOUR SUCCULENT PLANT

Succulents are a wide group that contains thousands of plants, both indoor and outdoor, making it impossible to classify a single genus and species. Succulent plants have several generic names that can be used interchangeably, making identification difficult. A individual may take a few steps to get a correct identification, which mostly rely on using the plant's physical characteristics as descriptors.

The Identification Process

Simply ask the plant seller which succulent plant is being purchased to prevent a lengthy identifying procedure. If the seller does not know or it is not practicable to inquire, begin by determining if the plant is a succulent or a cactus, and then narrowing down the species by examining the plant's leaf form and overall structure. First of all to differentiate a succulent from a cactus. Cactus plants generally have few or no leaves. We can recognize them thanks to the indentations, or areoles, along heir stems, from which the traditional spines spring.

Leaf Shape

From the large, thin, triangle-shaped leaves of an Aloe vera plant to the short, almost perfectly spherical leaves of a Senecio rowleyanus, also known as String of Pearls, succulents may have a wide range of leaf shapes. Knowing the leaf shape alone sometimes will help identify succulents quickly, especially in the case of succulents with very unusual leaf shapes, such as the String of Pearls.

Rosette Shape

The rosette form of succulent plants is characterized by tight clusters of leaves radiating out from a central point, almost like a rose. The leaves of some rosette succulents are pointed, while the leaves of others are rounded. I invite you to explore many of them, if you just stop and observe the many Echeverias in the market, you may be surprised of how much many of them look like beautiful mandalas.

Overall Configuration and Age

Succulents may have long stalks or strands, or they can be squat and close to the ground, rising outwards rather than upwards. Some succulents begin as a cluster of leaves poking out of the soil and develop into a tall, treelike structure with woody stems and leaves only on the plant's outermost parts, while others begin as a cluster of leaves poking out of the soil and grow into a tall, treelike structure with woody stems and leaves only on the plant's outermost parts. As a result, certain succulents can become easier to recognize as they develop and mature.

Plant Size

The average size of a plant will also aid in identification. Succulents that are either 2.8 to 3.1 inches (7 or 8 centimeters) tall or high are usually grown indoors, while bigger succulents are usually grown in a greenhouse. Plant size descriptors may assist a succulent owner in narrowing down their options.

Flower Color and Shape

If the succulent has distinguishing flowers, this detail may be helpful in determining its identity. The season in which the succulent blooms is also significant. Christmas cacti, for example, have long, colorful flowers with petals that bloom in early to mid-winter, typically just before Christmas, hence the term *"Christmas Cactus."*

Other Significant Details

There are a few other specifics that will assist in the detection of a succulent plant. If the plant has some easily described physical characteristics, such terms will serve as the plant's identification keywords. You most certainly have a Haworthiopsis attenuata or Haworthiopsis fasciata if you have a succulent with green, spiky leaves with white stripes. A plant owner can have a Sedum morganianum, also known as a Burro's Tail or Donkey's Tail, if the succulent plant has long, overlaying beanie leaves.

BEST INDOOR SUCCULENTS FOR YOUR HOUSE

In most cases, succulents make excellent indoor plants. They're low-maintenance, and since they're indigenous to sunny, dry climates, they're tolerant of a certain level of neglect. Echeveria or Jade plants are common choices for indoor succulent collections. They're like the entrance to the succulent kingdom. You'll certainly want to broaden your succulent horizons after you've had those for a while and maybe even propagated a few leaves here and there.

You will have the chance to select from a variety of exotic and unusual-looking succulent varieties. There are a plethora of eye-catching varieties to choose from, as well as strange and wonderful new leaves to begin your collection.

I already suggested you few succulents that areas to take care for in the above pages. I would like here to suggest you some very peculiar specimen, that would make you love this plants and will take your green passion to another level.

GENERAL SUCCULENT CARE

Let's start with some simple succulent care tips before we get into the unusual succulents I will be suggesting you. There are few general instructions for caring for succulents. Do however your due diligence on individual succulents to see if they need any special treatment.

• **Succulents Need Sunlight**: Most succulents prefer a hot, dry, and sunny environment in which to grow. Place the plant in a brightly lit area of your house. Choose the windowsill with the most sunlight. If you don't have enough natural light for your succulents, they can spread out in an attempt to reach the light. If this occurs, either bring the plant closer to the window or invest in a plant grow lamp. These lamps don't have to be costly and will provide enough light for your plant.

• **Succulents Don't Need So Much Water**: Succulents aren't used to a lot of rain and they're from hot climates. As a result, don't overwater your farm. You don't want succulents to sit in moist soil for too long and they're accustomed to dry conditions. Before watering, make sure the soil is fully dry. In the winter, use even less water. Succulents retain water in their leaves, allowing them to withstand drought.

• **Succulents Need Proper Drainage**: Succulents Need Proper Drainage: Choose a pot with drainage holes in the rim. This allows any extra water to drain after you've watered your succulent. Often, use cactus and succulent soil that drains well. You don't want the soil to be soggy. The roots thrive once the soil is well-drained.

FRITHIA PULCHRA

(Fairy Elephant Feet)

Frithia pulchra succulents are called "fairy elephant's feet" for a reason: their green leaves with translucent tips resemble tiny elephant feet. Frithia pulchra, like baby toes succulents, is a window succulent that has adapted well to the harsh grasslands it grows in.

It's not the easiest succulent to produce, but if you follow the instructions carefully, you shouldn't have any trouble keeping it alive.

Frithia pulchra has adapted to spend the most of its time partially underground in order to flourish in this harsh environment. The transparent leaf tips are often the only parts of the plant that are visible.

TRUST ME: They encourage light to penetrate deep into the leaf's sections that aren't exposed to direct sunlight.

Friry Elephant Feet Care Guide

LIGHT

The natural habitat of this succulent is very sunny. It will possibly take every light you give it in your house. Also direct sunlight should not be an issue, but you will need to dig the plant a little deeper into the substrate to prevent scorching..

TEMPERATURE

Frithia pulchra can withstand a wide range of temperatures, as one might imagine from such a hardy little succulent. In reality, if it's buried deep enough in the substrate so that only its leaf tips protrude, it should be able to withstand even the hottest summers.

The cold winters aren't a problem either. And light frost won't damage the plants as long as the soil is kept totally dry.

SENECIO BARBARTONICUS

(Himalaya)

Senecio Barbertonicus is a flowering succulent genus belonging to the Asteraceae family. Succulent Bush Senecio, Finger-leaved Senecio, Lemon Bean Bush, and Barberton Groundsel are all names for Senecio Barbertonicus.

Senecio barbertonicus Himalaya is a plant with densely packed, long, needle-like, bright green leaves and fragrant clusters of yellow tubular flowers. In urban interiors, these charming, spreading succulents add a touch of fun and texture. In the spring, expect little sparky yellow flowers.

Senecio Himalaya Care Guide

The succulent "Succulent Bush" is ideal for bringing variety and texture to container gardens and arrangements. Because of its height, this "Succulent Bush" will become heavy and tip over. Behead the top as it starts to flop until the stem is solid again.

LIGHT

From full light to partial light shade, the Barbertonicus will stay strong, until the light is bright and indirect. If you have the option to choose, a little early morning or late afternoon sun would work.

WATERING

Senecio is a drought-tolerant plant that stores water in its leaves. Allow the soil to dry out between waterings, yet do not overwater the plants or make them sit in water.

TEMPERATURE

Optimal room temperatures are 64 to 75F (18-24°C); but, when the plant is dormant during the winter, Senecio can withstand colder temperatures as low as 50F (10°C).

HEIGHT AND GROWTH

7-8 in (20-25cm) is the maximum height this plant can reach, and it will get taller slowly. Over the summer, apply a balanced fertilizer once a month.

CRASSULA RUPESTRIS MARNERIANA

Crassula Rupestris Marnieriana (or Hottentot) is a species of Crassula Rupestris. The Crassula plant family is likely familiar to succulent enthusiasts. Many of them are noteworthy for their peculiar leaf stacking and odd shapes. With clustered leaves arranged perfectly one on top of the other,

Crassula worm plants exemplify the fantastical arrangement of a living necklace.

TRUST ME: *The 'Hottentot' is a perfect little addition to any creepy and quirky set.*

Crassula Rupestris Care Guide

LIGHT

In their natural environment, they prefer direct sunshine all day, but as a house plant, they prefer bright but indirect light, rarely lying in direct morning or afternoon sunlight, trying to completely avoid direct sunlight during the midday sun. Exposed to direct sunlight, they will likely burn.

WATERING

Their succulent nature ensures the retention of water in its fleshy leaves, needing very little watering. When the soil is totally dry to the touch, water the vine. The easiest way to water it, is to hold the plant in its pot under flowing water while being careful not to get some water on the leaves themselves. Hold the pot over the sink and let the water soak into it until it no longer drips. After that, you should return it to its original location.

POTTING

Place your Crassula in a pot with plenty of drainage holes. Only the most seasoned succulent growers should attempt to plant them in a dish without a drainage hole, as overwatering or leaving them in moist conditions is the easiest way to destroy them. The roots will decay, and the plant will die as a result.

You won't need to water the plant again for another 2-3 weeks, maybe longer, based on the humidity level in your household. Regularly inspect the soil and then water the plant if the soil is totally dry to the touch.

The Crassula can be held in the same pot for many years. If it outgrows its container, replace it with a cactus and succulent compost that drains well and has a drainage medium like perlite.

GROWTH AND FLOWERING

In the spring and summer, this Crassula may produce a large number of small white or pink flowers.

FERTILIZER

From April to September, apply a succulent fertilizer 4-6 times.

XEROSICYOS DANGUYI

(Silver Dollar Plant)

Xerosicyos danguyi, also known as "Silver Dollar Plant," "Dollar Vine," or "Penny Plant," is a unique climbing succulent vine with dense, succulent, round silvery-green leaves and cylindrical roots. Climbing tendrils are found opposite the leaves, which are 1 to 2 inches long and thick.

Silver dollar vine, despite its appearance, belongs to the Cucurbitaceae family, which includes cucumbers. When the plant starts throwing out curly tendrils to catch and crawl with, you'll see the similarity. This means it begins its life on the ground and quickly scales higher objects, such as trees, in search of light. It may also become a pest, overtaking trees and making it difficult for them to grow fruit or even survive. On the other hand, Danguyi does not grow to be nearly as large or offensive as an indoor hoseplant.

Silver Dollar Plant Care Guide

WATERING

The Silver dollar is drought resistant. Actually when aggressively rising, Xerosicyos danguyi may take in more water. In cold weather, keep the soil drier to prevent root rot, just watering sufficiently to keep the leaves from shriveling.

USES

This is a unique succulent vine that scrambles up and hides fences, walls, and other obstacles. It may also be stored indoors in bright light as a hanging basket or container plant.

PROPAGATION

Soft wood cuttings can be used to propagate this plant by allowing them to callus over and then potting them up. It's even possible to grow it from seed. At 70°F (21°C), seeds germinate in 14-21 days. Plants that are cultivated from seed will form a caudex, but cuttings will not.

CRASSULA

(Buddha's Temple)

This is a special Crassula that I highly recommend. Also known as Buddha's Temple, it's a tall upright succulent with 'stacked' leaves columns that look like a Buddhist pagoda. At the top of each column, mature happy plants bear pompoms of pink flowers.

This Crassula succulent has a perfectly symmetrical tower appearance that would impress even the most pretentious succulent aficionado, making it look like a Buddhist shrine. Crassula CV. is a living sculpture that is also very easy to develop and care for.

Crassula Care Guide

LIGHT

The light Crassula plants prefer full sun over partial shade. During the hottest part of the day, however, the strong afternoon sun will burn the plants' leaves. If provided enough light, most Crassulas can be grown indoors.

TEMPERATUR

Crassula 'Buddha's Temple' can tolerate temperatures as low as 25 to 50 °F (-3.9 to 10 °C).

WATERING

Crassula plants need the same amount of water as other succulents. Overwatering can be avoided by using the "soak and dry" process, which involves soaking the soil in water, steadily draining it, and then allowing it to dry before watering again. In the winter, watering can be reduced.
Buddha's Temple Crassulas don't mind if the soil is acidic or alkaline, but they do like a porous, well-drained soil.

FERTILIZING

When Crassulas begin vigorously growing in mid-spring, they may benefit from a limited amount of organic fertilizer.

REPOTTING & PROPAGATION

Repot if required, preferably in the spring, at the start of an active growth cycle. Crassulas are usually propagated from stem or leaf cuttings. Seeds and offsets may also be used to cultivate them.

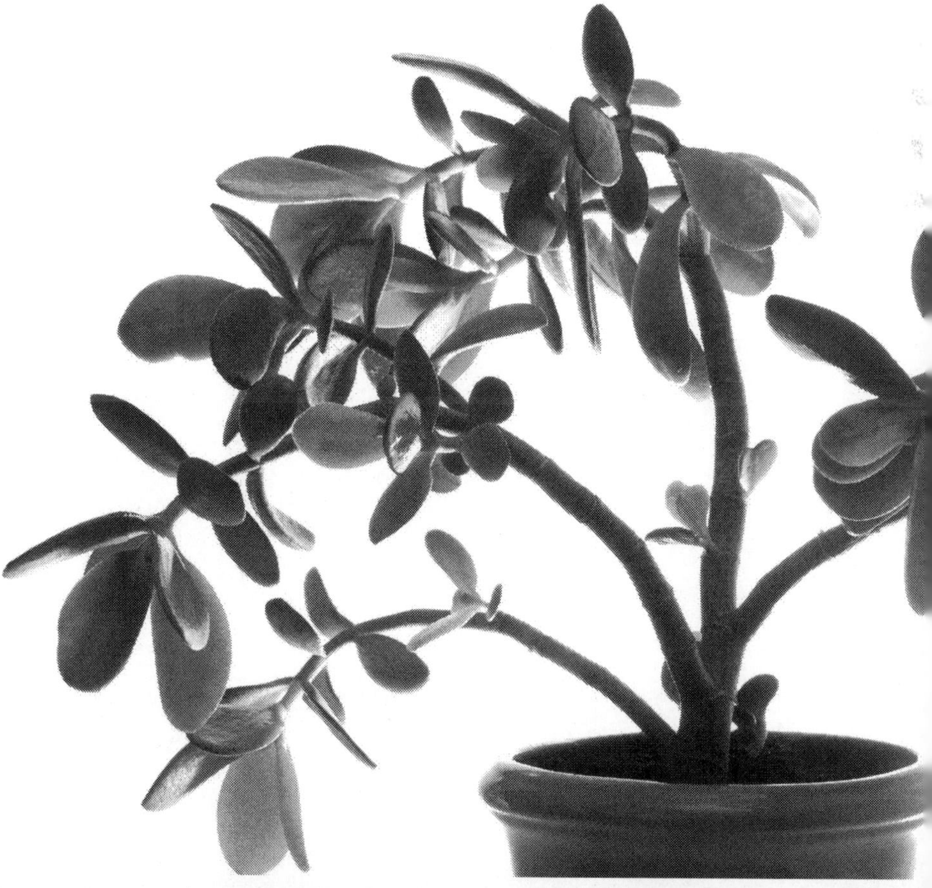

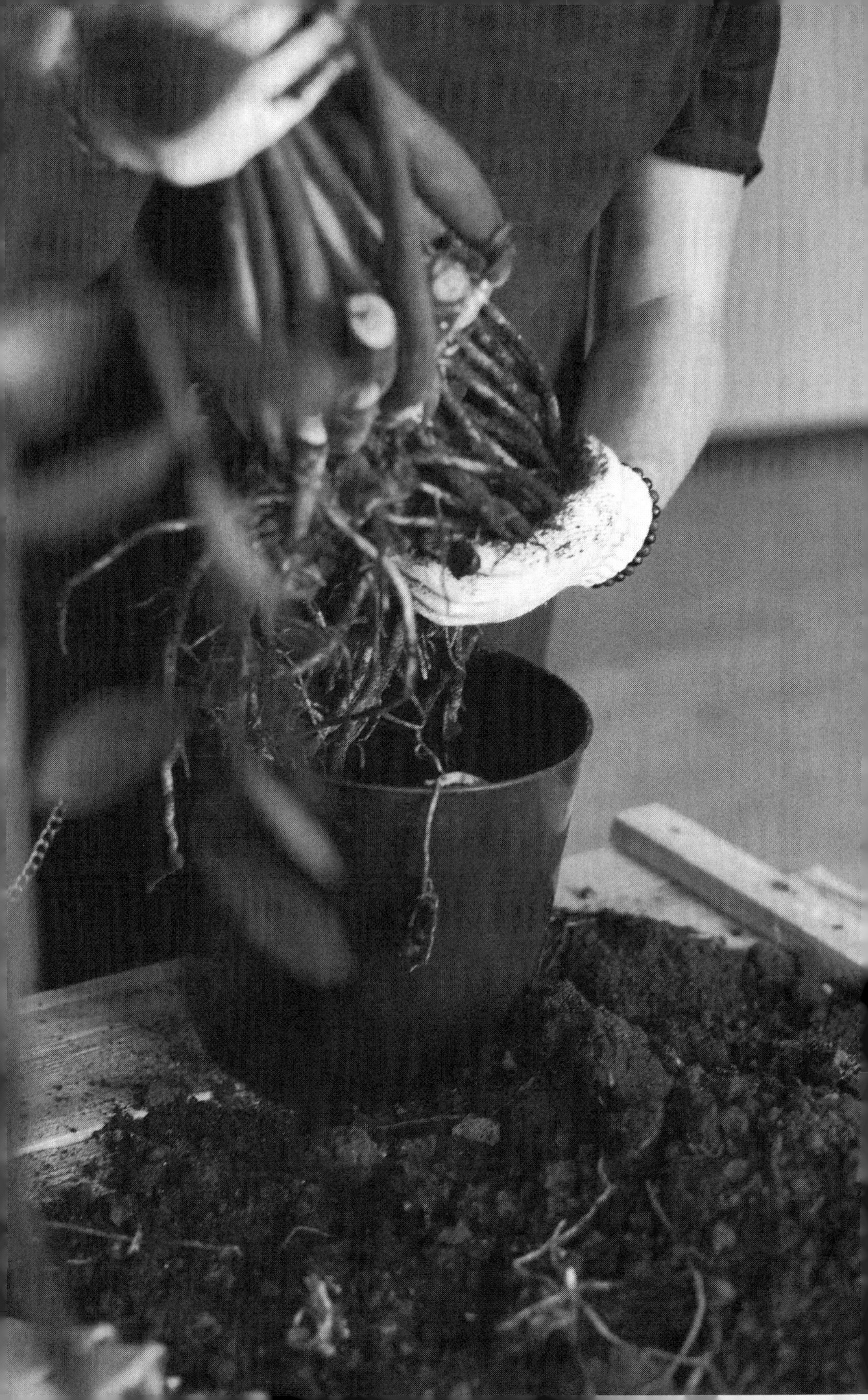

CHAPTER 4

Repotting Houseplants

Houseplants, which are once again fashionable, require repotting every year or two to stay stable and vigorous. Many of these plants emerge in the bleak rainforest floor, and although they've learned to deal with a lot of root rivalry, the confines of a pot will inevitably prove too much for them. Certain common houseplants, such as clivias, scheffleras, peace lilies, and ficus, prefer to be pot-bound, but still they may require repotting at some stage. It's the best time to do it now, at the outset of their annual growth cycle.

Apart from root congestion, plants that have been in a pot for so long are likely to be sitting in soil that has been compacted and polluted, as well as a dangerous buildup of fertilizer salts. When doing every sort of indoor plant treatment, including repotting, it's critical to examine each indoor plant individually.

The frequency of potting up (transplanting seedlings), repotting, or simply providing a soil adjustment is a significant factor that varies depending on the species and its condition. Repotting entails washing up, perhaps pruning roots, and replenishing soil, while 'potting up' refers to the process of transplanting seedlings.

The word 'potting on' is often used to describe transplanting to a larger pot.

HOW DO YOU TELL WHETHER A PLANT NEEDS REPOTTING?

Turn the pot over; roots coming out of the drainage holes is the most visible indicator of a pot-bound plant. Remove the plant's lower stem from the container with a tight grip. It's time to act if you see a thicket of pale roots in the form of the pot. If the pot won't come off, it's more likely due to clogged roots. You should take the jar out from the pot if it's made of plastic. If it's mud, you will need to use a hammer to smash it up.

Another symptom of a concern is whether the plant seems to be thirsty all of the time, wilting through regular watering. This is because the root-to-soil ratio has become too high. The same issue will result in a noticeable decrease in plant vigor.

To reduce the burden of the ordeal and make the roots more workable, water the plant deeply the day before repotting.

BENEFITS OF REPOTTING

The benefits of repotting for our indoor plants' health can be enormous. More space for plants to thrive, more air reaching the root system, preventing weak soil and roots from being root bound, resulting in loss of growth and waterlogged soil, more important nutrients provided, and disease prevention are only a few of the advantages.

WHEN TO REPOT

• Springtime

Repotting is expected for the majority of indoor plants in the spring, and it's best done just before or when new growth appears. Because of the longer daylight hours, more heat, and warmer temperatures, this is a good time for new development.

Other plants on the other hands, like winter flowering species and bulbs that go dormant in the autumn, are not suitable for spring repotting. These plants should be repotted during fall. You should check the care directions for your specific plant.

TRUST ME: Check the quality and condition of all plants in the house at the start of the year. If you see that they need pruning, repotting, or some other kind of treatment, make a note of it for each plant. It's a fantastic way to prepare ahead of time. This is also a good time to prune if necessary.

• New Potted Plants

Many house plants need to be repotted when they first get home, unless you feel they've been well cared for and the soil and pot size are right.

It's not rare to purchase plants that are in bad health, and need repotting. To avoid more shock from changes in the conditions and climate, repotting should be performed after a week or two of the plant settling into the house.

• Root/Pot bound

When roots have outgrown their current pot, the word "root bound" or "pot bound" is used to indicate that it's time to try a larger pot. The classic 'roots growing through the drainage holes' and roots growing in a circular fashion since they have no space to expand, are signs of too much root for the pot. Keep in mind that certain plants, especially flowering varieties, benefit from a certain amount of close fitting inside a pot, which allows them to bloom more effectively (African violets are a good example).

You should remove the plant and see if it's pot bound from the outside of the pot if you're not sure. It won't hurt you, and you can return it until you've checked the roots.

• **Plant or Pot Problems**

When a plant becomes pot bound, it may expand slowly or not at all. But first, check for underfeeding, overwatering, or a lack of light. Root bound can be identified by the soil drying out quickly.

When hard water is used or overfeeding is done, white ice-like forms on the outside edge of a clay pot, and a green slime forms as a result of blocked drainage or the plant being overwatered. Both would necessitate pot removal, potential repotting, fresh soil, and sterilization of the old pot.

STEPS OF REPOTTING

• **Step 1 - Prepare the Pots**

It's a smart idea to scrub the pots thoroughly before sterilizing them with a 10% chlorine solution. This is done in order to keep plant pathogens at bay. It's worth giving terracotta pots a good soak for a couple of hours to eliminate the clay's dryness, allowing the fresh soil and plant to absorb as many of the nutrients as possible outside of the pot.

The controversy about whether to place terracotta, crock pieces, or other materials in the bottom of the pot has been with us since forever.

The biggest advantage of putting material in the bottom of a pot may be improved drainage and the avoidance of root rot caused by waterlogged soil. When a plant prefers to draw water from the bottom of the pot, where there is no dirt, some farmers are afraid that insects may have better access to the plant (the bottom can have a small covering with tiny holes to solve this).

Plastic pots for plants that need a lot of drainage can benefit from crocking, and containers without drainage would need a layer of pebbles.

• Step 2 - Removing from the Pot

Plants can be difficult to extract from containers, particularly if they've been root bound and have spent much time inside them. If everything else fails, crack the pot if it's clay or hack into plastic rather than yanking the plant out, which may cause major problems.

To remove soil from plastic potted plants, pressing the sides of the container gently loosens the soil, then turn the plant on its side and slip it out. Nine times out of ten, this will do. Clay potted plants can be more difficult to deal with as they cannot be squeezed. You may need to use a butter knife to loosen them up by running it between the soil edge and the pot wall. If you're having trouble removing anything, look and see if any roots are emerging into the drainage holes. If this is the case, force them inward with a blunt object wider than the drainage hole or hack them out with a sharp knife.

TRUST ME: It's good to gently ease the plant out by keeping it at the bottom of the stem with your hand in the dirt, but you must be very patient to know what plant you're dealing with. Woody and strong stems are easier, but some stems are so gentle you could snap your plant from the root ball easily.

Root Preparation: When the plant is out of its old container, inspect the root system and cut away any weakened or unnecessary roots. It is beneficial to remove some of the old dirt from the root ball. This is accomplished by massaging along the root ball's outer side and, in some cases, merely removing extra soil.

• Step 3 - Fertilizer

Fertilize the plant with a soluble all-purpose fertilizer that has been refined according to the label's instructions. Examine the plant to see if it needs repotting. Remember that once you've pruned the plant's leaves, it'll actually take less water than before, so change accordingly.

Within a week or two, you should see new development. Pinch out rising tips to facilitate branching until new shoots have two sets of leaves, then repeat on subsequent branches.

• Step 4 - Potting

When you've chosen a pot, washed it, selected the proper potting mix, and have a plant without a pot that's ready to be transplanted, just fill the bottom of the fresh pot with enough dirt.

When you can put the plant on top of the bottom soil with the plant stem and the beginning of the root segment sitting at the correct level with the rim of the container, you've got the right spot (allow a few millimeters or so gap below the rim for ease of watering).

It's time to fill in the margins, between the roots and the pot wall, until the location is right, and you're satisfied with the height the plant is sitting at.

It's helpful to gently drive your thumbs into the dirt, just don't overdo it and compact the soil to the point that air and water can't circulate freely. If future watering cause the soil to compress, you can still apply more top soil. You will not have enough root system to seat the plant after the first stage of filling the pot with soil. And that's perfect. Simply use the bottom soil to gauge the level and fill in the edges as best you can.

• Step 5 - Water, Care and Relax

Now that you've completed the task, all that's left to do is to supply the repotted house plants with their favorite beverage: water. The majority of plants would need a thorough watering from the surface, allowing water to seep into the whole soil and root system, followed by 30 minutes of no additional water from the pot saucer. If the soil sinks too far after being watered, simply top it up.

When the plant is healing from the transplant, keep it out of direct sunlight and don't fertilizer for at least a month (new potting mix should have plenty of nutrients anyway).

Overwatering may cause sagging and limp leaves or roots, and if they turn yellow, you might be overwatering. You will relax as the plants absorb the new nutrients and thrive in their new space.

HOW TO PICK THE PERFECT POT

Have you ever believed you found the right pot for your houseplant, only to find it was completely wrong until you put it inside the container?

Plants are a kind of living being. Plants are delicate and have subtle characteristics that make them deserving of being the center of attention, and matching them with the right planters necessitates some consideration and preparation.

It may be difficult to ignore your beloved colors and patterns, but the colors and patterns you put on your body or paint on your walls will not be the same as the colours and patterns you see on the walls. Let's take a look at the fundamentals of selecting the best pots for our houseplants!

1. Hot Plants

Some plants have a vivid, shiny, and neon quality to them. Others have deep, rich tones that take center stage. Using neutral earth tones or monochromatic colours such as white, black, or grey can help to concentrate attention on your plants. These shades are also compatible with most home décor palettes, so you won't have to worry about clashing with your prized velvet emerald sofa! If you like bright colours, consider introducing colours that complement rather than clash with your plants.

2. Playful Patterns

Planting smaller houseplants in larger pots is a common mistake because certain plants grow slowly. Choose a plant pot that is the right size for the plant. Your smaller plants will tend to be larger and more full as a result of this!

3. Optical Illusions

Planting smaller houseplants in larger pots is a common mistake because certain plants grow slowly. Choose a plant pot that is the right size for the plant. Your smaller plants will tend to be larger and more full as a result of this!

4. Hang In There

Use vining plants to soften hard angles if you prefer tall, elongated planters. Unlike tall plants in tall planters, which appear to project a stark, blunt focal point, the foliage will spill over the sides, forming a gentle wave.

CONCLUSION

Keeping indoor plants in decent physical condition is probably not the easiest of the hobbies, but taking care of such diverse, brautiful, happiness-gifting living beings can be the healthiest of the medicines for our everyday busy lives. This guide has been created with he aim to give you a no-fuss useful informations to give you an introduction to select some of the greatest green friends we could introduce into our homes.

All these plants can thrive indoors without a lot of light, air, or water. Indoor plants grow at a slower rate than those that grow outdoors and this allow us to keep them under control and make them be a nice addendum to our living spaces.

Of course you will have to make everything in your power to make your house a comfortable environment for them, for example keeping under check the air dryness. Especially during winter there may be a lack of moisture between the walls of our houses so we should help the plants keeping the humidity up or watering them more often, with chlorine-less water (just leave the tap-water in a bottle for a few days before using it to water your plants- and don't use the last bit of it).

Just using few precautions you can make your green thumb greener beef you can even realize it. I'd sugget you to start with your favorite two plant from this book. Just two, focus on them as they were your pets. Observe them and try to notice every little change in their shape, color, position, density, and adjust accordingly to their reaction. Observation is always the strongest tool when it comes to deal with another living being and plants are no different.

Give them some love and they will make your world a brighter place.

C.

INDEX

Aechmea Fasciata	97
African Violet	13
Aglaonema	15
Alocasia	21
Aloe Barbadensis	25
Bird of Paradise	32
Bird's Nest Fern	29
Boston Fern	35
Cactus	38
Chlorophytum	89
Chrysanthemum Morifolium	79
Crassula ovata	67
Crassula Rupestris Marneriana	120
Crassula	125
Cyclamen Persicum	105
Dypsis Lutescens	27
Echeverias	53
Epipremnum Aureum	82
Frithia pulchra	116
Hedera Helix	62
Hoya Kerrii	91
Jasminum polyanthum	65
Jewel Orchid	71
Kala choe Blossfeldiana	57
Maculata Begonia	10
Monstera Deliciosa	74
Musa	47
Oxalis	85
Phalaenopsis	77
Plectranthus Scutellarioides	44
Schlumbergera Buckleyi	41
Schlumbergera Gaertneri	50
Senecio Barbartonicus	118
Spathiphyllum	60
Tillandsia Air Plants	18
Tillandsia	95
Tradescantia Zebrina	100
Xerosicyos danguyi	123
Zamioculcas Zamiifolia	102

Make sure to not miss out on my first contribution to the Houseplant world where you will learn how to pot, grow and groom your plants at home:
The Houseplants Guide for Beginners and Plant Lovers: *A Comprehensive Book to Choose, Grow, and Live Better with Your Indoor Plants*

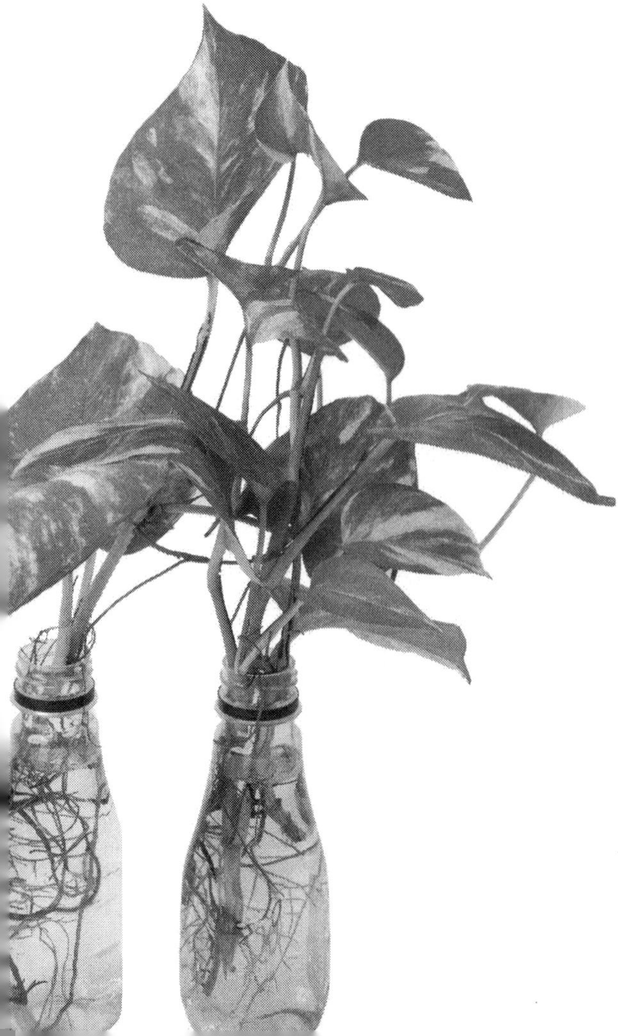